"Judy is a master at helping people to transform conflict into powerful relationships. Her very useful guide will provide the tools to change intractable situations into high-level teamwork and unimaginable possibilities. Let Judy teach you to dance on the ever-shifting carpet of relationships."

—Thomas Crum, author of *Three Deep Breaths,*
Journey to Center, and *The Magic of Conflict*

"Workplaces are designed for conflict. They bring together competing interests of customers, designers, marketers, engineers, manufacturers, and budgets. This book provides practical and easily implemented ways to allow these conflicts to be productive and relationship-building. I highly recommend the book and hope that its insights leak into the larger arena of our civic and political dialogue. In the end, our way of life may depend on our capacity to trust and cooperate with strangers. The ideas in this book take us in that direction."

—Peter Block, author of *Flawless Consulting,*
Stewardship, and *Community*

"When two people don't get along, you can't just put them into a room and hope for the best, or assign them to a project and insist they work together. All relationships have some conflict, and some relationships are subject to deep conflicts. Addressing destructive behavior related to conflict is important. And addressing conflict when it happens, in a way that builds connection, collegiality, and allows individuals to share vulnerabilities takes time and nurturing. Judy Ringer has a way of working with individuals in conflict so that the relationship (assuming all parties want this) becomes healthy. That said, we need conflict! But we don't need destructive behavior that sometimes accompanies conflict. Anyone in business can tell you that individuals with healthy relationships, even in the midst of conflict, create a highly productive and psychologically safe environment at work, when they know how to work through the conflict appropriately. Judy's work provides solid recommendations, practical advice, and methods to address conflict; the book provides great insights to help rid organizations of behavior and approaches that can harm or destroy relationships."

—Connie Roy-Czyzowski, SPHR, SHRM-SCP, CCP,
vice president of human resources, Northeast Delta Dental

"This brilliant book has a wealth of material: insights, processes, and practices for anyone who is engaged in coaching people who don't get along. Judy offers powerful tools using concepts and principles taken from the martial art of aikido. Drawing from her experience on the aikido mat and as a coach in organizations, she has laid out the coaching process in clear, concise, and accessible steps that will help anyone move from conflict toward resolution. I appreciate that her intention is to go beyond organizational coaching, she is also emphasizing "teaching skills that will support the parties ever after in all areas of life." A great contribution.

—Wendy Palmer, author of *Leadership Embodiment*

"Judy Ringer's book is for leaders who want to empower themselves to manage workplace conflict. Imagine being fearless when conflict arises, and having the tools and confidence you need to address, manage, and guide your team toward peace and organizational health."

—Fran Liautaud, organizational development
and training manager

"*Turn Enemies Into Allies* is a powerful guide to proactively deal with conflict in the workplace. There is a definite 'cost' to avoiding conflict, which will be reduced by following the sage advice offered by Judy Ringer. She skillfully takes the reader through concrete steps and offers exceptional examples from her years of experience. As a management consultant and professor, I found myself reflecting on situations in my life and thought if I had this book, the conflict would have been resolved much quicker and with less drama for all parties involved. *Turn Enemies Into Allies* is truly a gift to new and seasoned managers!"

—Susan Losapio, PhD, professor, Southern New Hampshire
University School of Business

Enemies

TURN •

INTO

Allies

THE ART OF PEACE IN THE WORKPLACE

JUDY RINGER

Foreword by James Warda
Illustrations by Adam Richardson

CAREER
PRESS

This edition first published in 2019 by Career Press, an imprint of
Red Wheel/Weiser, LLC
With offices at:
65 Parker Street, Suite 7
Newburyport, MA 01950
www.redwheelweiser.com
www.careerpress.com

ISBN: 978-1-63265-154-9
Library of Congress Cataloging-in-Publication Data
available upon request.

Cover design by Robert Johnson
Interior photos/images by Adam Richardson
Interior by Gina Schenck
Typeset in Adobe Garamond Pro and Arial Narrow

Printed in Canada
MAR
10 9 8 7 6 5 4 3 2 1

Dedicated to Lorna Metskas
Mother, teacher, and biggest ally.
Thank you.

Your job is to create a work environment that
enables the success of the people who work with you,
and if conflict is not resolved effectively, you can never hope
to keep your good staff. So have a go and see what happens;
you may be better at it than you think.

—SeeChange Consulting

CONTENTS

Phase 3: Redirecting (Joint Sessions)

Phase 4: Bowing Out

FOREWORD

Writing a foreword is an awesome responsibility.

Now, by "awesome," I don't only mean "great," though it is definitely that.

I also mean it's important. And significant. And, if you think too long about it, a tad bit overwhelming as you realize you want to get it just right.

Yes, writing a foreword is an awesome responsibility because, in doing so, you are accountable for sharing something and someone important with the world. And, like the bearer of any special gift, you need to show it in the best light possible. Think diamond ring in a velvet box.

Now, if you asked Judy Ringer if she considers herself to be a gift, she'd probably roll her eyes. That's because she's humble. And that humility is an essential part of *Turn Enemies Into Allies*. Because nothing can humble us more quickly than conflict, and demonstrating humility is also essential to making your way through it.

Of course, like most, I used to avoid conflict. I hated the teeth-grinding, stomach-churning guts of it. But Judy helped me see it more as something to embrace, knowing that, when I come out the other side, I'll be stronger and hopefully wiser.

Interestingly, I first found Judy the way you'd expect to find someone or something incredibly important.

I did a Google search.

I was searching because I'd run out of ideas. As the manager of a large corporate team, I was looking for help in dealing with a challenging business partner. I had already talked to several colleagues, read some books and articles, and even watched a few videos. But nothing was giving me what I needed. So I searched.

And, in doing so, I came across Judy's work. Then, two coincidences, one right away and the other later, made me pay even closer attention.

First, I saw that the name of her blog was *Ki Moments,* describing those moments, in her words, as those "in which you are fully aware of your life force and your ability to influence your environment."

As someone who writes about moments myself, that definitely rang a bell. Several, in fact.

Coincidence number one.

Through Judy's work, I found valuable guidance in how to approach my business partner in an open and curious way, starting with listening instead of talking. And, using what she taught, within a few conversations, he and I actually ended up laughing together about our children. After experiencing that kind of transformation, I began sharing what I had learned from Judy with my team.

Soon though, I faced what, for me, was an even tougher situation. Two of the key people on my team weren't working well together. And, if they didn't work well together, my entire team couldn't. So, I started rummaging again for tools in my leadership "toolkit," having them meet regularly, working with them to create shared goals, assigning them training, and so and so on. But none of it worked well, or for long.

That is when I learned that Judy had recently completed a manuscript for *Turn Enemies Into Allies,* a book that appeared to address the same issue I was facing. Again.

Coincidence number two.

After offering to write the book's foreword because of my belief in Judy's message, reinforced by the difference her work had made for me personally, I had the privilege of reading the actual manuscript. And, once again, I was pleasantly surprised to find the exact approach

I needed. This time, to help my two team members through and beyond their present situation. And, at the same time, teach them skills that they'd be able to use elsewhere at work, at home, and basically anywhere conflict might arise.

One final thought. In reading this book, I believe you're going to also have your own pleasant surprise. Namely, Judy doesn't talk "at" you, but "with" you. As if you're sitting down with a friend. And what makes this friend extra special is that she brings not only a depth and breadth of experience in conflict management, but a passion for aikido. A passion that is clearly evident as she weaves the martial art's concepts and terms throughout the book.

So, with that, I'll let you open your gift. The following pages await.

And, after you finish and start applying its lessons, notice what happens in and around you. Your life will change. And change other lives as a result.

In that way, this is one case in which regifting isn't just tolerated, it's encouraged.

Take care,
James Warda
Author of *Where Are We Going So Fast?:*
Finding the Sacred in Everyday Moments

Harmony doesn't mean getting along with people at any cost just to avoid a confrontation. Harmony as used in aikido does not involve compromising at all. Rather aikido's harmony brings different, even opposing, elements together and intensifies them in a way that drives everything toward a higher level.

—Mitsunari Kanai, *Technical Aikido*

Introduction

Does this path have a heart? If it does, the path is good; if it doesn't, it is of no use.... For me there is only the traveling on paths that have heart . . . and there I travel looking, looking, breathlessly.
—Don Juan, A Yaqui warrior, as told to Carlos Castaneda

Always practice the Art of Peace in a vibrant and joyful manner.
—Morihei Ueshiba, founder of aikido

There are many, many concepts from the martial art aikido I've incorporated into my life, and one of the most useful is the awareness that I am always giving and receiving *ki*—Japanese for "energy" or "life force." I am giving and receiving whether I mean to or not. Over time, I've learned to see not an attack and not even people, but energy. And with time, I've learned to be more intentional about the energy I give, express, and extend to others as well as how I manage what comes my way.

On the aikido mat, it's inevitable that some partners are easy to work with and others are not. In life, too, sometimes the dance is easy. We enjoy our partners as we flow together through life, work, and relationships. Other times, the dance is fraught with missteps, interference, collisions, and falls. The flow is interrupted by our inability to see ourselves as contributors. We know we can't move, but we don't know why. We're caught in patterns we are often unaware of.

Aikido helps us see our part in creating the dance. We learn to be intentional on the mat. We learn to relax when we wish our partner would relax. We understand that if we're forcing the technique, it's time to stop and try something different. Off the mat as well, I begin to see what I can and cannot control. Instead of avoiding or resisting the energy coming my way, I learn to dance with it, harness it, and guide it. Erstwhile enemies become dance partners and potential allies.

This book is a guide for managing and resolving conflict in the workplace. It is also a guide for managing conflict in all areas of life. And our complex world needs it. We need guides in the form of human beings—like you—who understand that in conflict, there is always a choice point. When two roads diverge, do I give in to the triggers that lead to high drama, reactions, and regret? Or do I choose the centered path of awareness, connection, and purpose?

We get better at what we practice—another lesson from aikido. Psychologist Chris Argyris, who gave us the Ladder of Inference, called it "skilled incompetence"—the notion that we are, in fact, practicing all the time even when the results are not what we want. Our daily thoughts and actions are well-traveled neural pathways that can be reinforced or restructured with intention.

Personally, I want to practice intentionally. So if my path is not leading me where I want to go, I can stop, reflect, and choose a new one.

You will change, too, as you practice what you teach. Conflict, like life, is a learning path. Be curious and easy with yourself as you find your way as a teacher of conflict resolution skills. Enjoy watching the interactions of the participants as well as your own. Always keep a sense of humor. And find the path with heart.

I hope you're ready to take on a workplace challenge. I hope the principles and framework offered here give you a path to follow. And I hope you always practice in a vibrant and joyful manner.

Why Should You Read This Book?

What should I do when coworkers don't get along? In a quarter-century of training and coaching, I've seen dozens of managers and leaders struggle with this question. As a conflict and communication skills professional, I work closely with managers of small businesses and corporate teams. Usually, the manager asks me to solve the problem—

to intervene between two people who are equally important to the company and who are not getting along. In many cases, their conflict is distracting to those around them and hurting the organization.

When I ask the manager to describe the problem, common responses include:

- ✍ "There's a personality conflict between two key players that needs resolving."
- ✍ "I don't know what to do with coworkers who can't get along."
- ✍ "When do I let people work it out themselves, and when do I get involved?"
- ✍ "Their conflict is disrupting our workflow/customer service/ productivity/team."

I understand the manager's challenge. Although intervening in conflict is not for the faint of heart, it comes with the job if you're a manager, supervisor, or leader. Even so, you may not have received the necessary training or previously encountered such a challenge.

The first time I was asked to mediate and resolve a workplace conflict between two employees, I was hesitant. At the time, my work centered on training individuals and groups in addressing conflict, engaging in difficult conversations, and overcoming performance anxiety. I was experienced in mediation techniques, but I sensed this request called for something different. The client wanted these employees to be able to work well together beyond the resolution of the current conflict. Most of the problems I see emanate from a lack of awareness and skill. If the parties had the skills, they could resolve any conflict—the current one and those that might arise in the future.

In addition, the word "mediation" has a formal quality to it, with accompanying rules, definitions, and conditions, and often evokes a legal or courtroom mindset, causing people to tighten, distance themselves from the process, and revert to a contest mentality. Also, as a mediator, you generally follow prescribed formats, and although the parties gain skill through participating in the mediation, the primary goal of the mediator is not necessarily to teach but to act as an intermediary and interpreter, and to facilitate agreements.

When I work one-on-one with individuals, I call it "conflict coaching," and I heard this request as exactly that: Coach two individuals, one at a time, in the same conflict management skills and aikido concepts central to my group trainings, until they're able to sit together and talk to each other about rebuilding their working relationship. In many ways, this approach offers a middle ground between mediation and conflict coaching. As in mediation, agreement and resolution are the desired outcome. Here, equally important is the emphasis on teaching skills that will support the parties ever after in all areas of life.

As I fielded more of these requests to work with individuals in conflict, I confirmed my sense that the work was about instructing people on the needed skills to sort things out. If the individuals were interested, motivated, and willing to acquire the skills, there was every reason to believe the individuals themselves would resolve the conflict. What's more, the parties could walk away with expertise and leadership qualities to apply in other settings—a win for the employees, their manager, and the organization.

This Book Is a Process and a Guide

This book is a precise and practical guide for catching employee conflict before it escalates and coaching the parties to resolution. It is a process I developed to help two individuals resolve conflict, communicate more effectively, and rebuild a working relationship. As I refined and developed the process over time, I became convinced that managers and leaders could do what I did and achieve similar results.

This guide offers a deliberate and methodical way of working with employees in conflict—an approach that draws on my expertise in conflict and communication skill-building as well as my training in mind-body principles from aikido. In my experience, managers, supervisors, and human resource (HR) professionals receive limited preparation for dealing with employee conflict—even though this is a fact of life in their work. Research published in the October 1, 2016, issue of *Forbes* reveals that 98 percent of managers believe they need more training to deal effectively with "important issues such as professional development, conflict resolution, employee turnover, time management and project management."

Dealing with conflict is an essential element of management, and yet one that many managers avoid. Conflict can be hard, complex, and fraught with emotional roadblocks. If you find yourself stuck in this mindset, it's harder to see the benefits of conflicting views, such as the advantage that multiple perspectives bring to the solution of a problem.

However, with a shift in perspective, an investment of time and practice, and the clearly defined four-phase model in this book, you'll be able to manage the majority of workplace conflicts and help members of your team build key skills. At the same time, you'll reap personal and professional benefits from exploring new ideas, experimenting, and being open to learning.

In addition, while this method is highly valuable as a managerial intervention with conflicting employees, it also offers skills and tools just as useful in the executive suite as they are in the family kitchen. As a result, this approach is effective across organizational strata—at the executive level, with middle management, or on employee teams. Anyone with influence can initiate the process. You can invite the conflicting parties into the conversation yourself or find a neutral party to help you.

The Costs of Unaddressed Conflict

As tempting as it may be to ignore interpersonal conflict, addressing it is important for organizations for a host of reasons.

At the top of the list, unaddressed conflict is costly. A 2008 study commissioned by CPP, Inc.—authors of personality and conflict style assessments such as the Myers-Briggs Type Indicator (MBTI) and Thomas-Kilmann (TKI) conflict mode instrument—found that 85 percent of employees at all levels of the surveyed organizations experienced conflict to varying degrees. The study also found that in the United States, an average employee spends nearly three hours a week dealing with workplace conflict. At the time of the study, those hours amounted to approximately $359 billion in hourly wages.

Secondly, conflict among coworkers saps energy and limits creativity. I see otherwise skilled and technically savvy managers and executives stymied when faced with team members who aren't working together productively. In a 2012 survey of HR professionals by UK author and mediator Marc Reid, the most negative aspects of conflict in the workplace were found to be the distress it causes employees (45 percent) and the fact that it distracts from business objectives (34 percent). Two-thirds responded that it "impacts operational performance of the company."

These clear consequences mean the situation can't be avoided. If you intervene unskillfully, you will make the problem worse. If you ignore the issue, it usually remains unresolved and negatively impacts the work environment. Good people leave. Work is done inefficiently because coworkers won't talk to each other. Relationships and output suffer, and entire organizations become polarized. According to the CPP study, 43 percent of employees think their bosses don't deal with conflict well.

The good news is, while not always intuitive, the skills and competencies to resolve organizational conflict can be learned. Learning to intervene intelligently in workplace conflict saves you and your team money and time, and reduces stress levels. You'll also give the conflicting parties the opportunity to build emotional intelligence and confidence, and watch as they pass these competencies on to others. Managers and leaders who demonstrate the confidence and ability to address conflict foster happier, more productive, and more inclusive workplaces. We spend too much of our lives at work for the environment to be otherwise.

A New Approach

My approach to conflict stems from the martial arts, specifically the Japanese martial art aikido. In 1994, I started practicing aikido because I resonated with the metaphor it offers for dealing with difficulty, challenge, and the unexpected. Usually, people think I discovered the martial art first, and that led to my training and coaching career, when actually it was the other way around. A conflict—and my desire to improve my own communication style—led me to aikido and to this work.

For fourteen years, I sold residential real estate. Real estate transactions can be contentious. I often found myself in the middle of a heated contest between buyer and seller, or with the need to advocate for a transaction with a banker, building inspector, or concerned family member. My default conflict style is to accommodate other people's wishes, and that isn't always useful in those kinds of transactions.

The clash that ultimately drove me to become a student of conflict was with the manager of an agency I worked for. She had a strong need to control, and I was used to a lot of freedom. I almost left the company because I couldn't express to the new manager that her style felt smothering to me. Luckily, a leader higher up the ladder saw my unhappiness and my foot moving toward the door. He sent me to a weeklong program he'd previously attended.

During that training, I was introduced to aikido and its countless applications, including its use in addressing conflict, solving problems, and determining one's purpose. I met author, aikidoist, and presenter Thomas Crum, who became a mentor and lifelong friend. Tom had been teaching aikido since the early 1970s. Along with other aikidoists—such as Terry Dobson and George Leonard—Tom combined aikido with his life as a trainer and educator, and was among the first to apply the essential principles of aikido to work and family conflict. His books inspired me to continue along that path, and his trainings changed the direction of my life.

In 1993, I formed Power & Presence Training, and within a year had founded my own aikido school with help from instructors at nearby aikido centers. Happily, Portsmouth Aikido is alive and well today, currently owned by one of my original students. I'm a third-degree black belt and member of the board of directors.

Aikido: The Art of Peace

Aikido is first and foremost a martial art. It has roots in judo and jujutsu, and yet is quite different in that the goal is not to block a strike, win a contest, or otherwise prevail over an opponent.

Aikido is a fairly recent evolution of the martial arts, developed in the early twentieth century by Morihei Ueshiba, a highly skilled and renowned Japanese swordsman and martial artist. The word *aikido* is often translated as "the way of blending or harmonizing with energy" or more simply "the Art of Peace." Aikido principles, such as entering—moving off the line of the attack and into a partnering relationship with the attacker—create alignment with the incoming energy, or ki.

Another principle is blending. When you enter and align with the incoming energy, you can blend with it—add your energy to it. Next is redirecting the energy such that both attacker and receiver remain unharmed. These three principles—entering, blending, and redirecting—are fundamental to aikido as well as to our four-phase process, and we will return to them often.

Aikido principles are taught and used throughout the world to de-escalate conflict as well as build stability, flexibility, and presence. Because aikido involves more flowing than fighting, most students begin with the goal of learning a martial art that teaches self-defense without injuring others. Students soon understand the physical components of the art apply in the outside world as well.

In aikido, an attack is reframed as power that can be developed and guided. Consequently, the aikidoist does not block or hinder the opponent. Our first move is to enter. We want to find our partner's energy, and join or blend with it. What would normally be understood as an act of aggression is instead seen as energy to be utilized—entered into, blended with, and redirected—changing the dynamic from resistance to connection.

Similarly, the parties in the four-phase intervention described in this book learn to enter a difficult conversation by listening first. Through active listening, they gain valuable information, and begin to understand their opponent/partner's feelings, needs, and objectives. Then, the parties *blend* by acknowledging and appreciating their partner's view. They *redirect* their partner's energy by offering their own view and focusing the conflict energy on solutions that are mutually beneficial.

When I'm with workshop participants, or coaching clients to resolve a conflict, I introduce them to the martial art and the metaphor, and then invite them to partner in aikido movements that simulate the stated problem. Through visual and kinesthetic experiences, both parties gain insight into their behavioral patterns and, more importantly, how they might respond more effectively.

By practicing hands-on exercises as well as developing an understanding of the underlying aikido intention of disarming without harm through entering, blending, and redirection, individuals and organizations regain composure and move from adversarial to partnering relationships. When conflict is reframed as a normal part of life that can be skillfully managed and transformed, relationships mend, and team members learn to discuss and resolve issues rather than avoid them.

An Aikido Lexicon

In my twenty-five-plus years of practicing aikido, I've come to see the world so thoroughly through the aikido lens that I sometimes forget that others don't speak this language. Here are a few key words and phrases from my aikido practice, and how I use them in this book:

- ☙ **On the mat:** Aikidoists practice on a firm but springy mat so we can learn how to take the beautiful falls aikido is known for. We fall down and get up again approximately 150 times a night. Falling and bouncing back is one way we blend with and receive our partner's energy. When we're "on the mat," we're learning techniques, so I use this phrase when I'm speaking about actual physical aikido or the metaphorical "mat" of the coaching session.

- ☙ **Off the mat:** I use this phrase when talking about the opportunities life offers to practice aikido verbally and relationally every day. When I find myself in a difficult life situation, I practice "off the mat" aikido. I ask myself, "Am I trying to win an argument at any cost, or am I interested in hearing my conflict partner out so that we can try and reach an agreement?" "Am I perceiving feedback as criticism or as potentially useful information?" "How do I blend with and redirect a verbal insult?"

- ☙ **Ki:** Translations of this word include "energy," "power," and "life force." It is the Japanese equivalent of *ch'i*, as in *tai ch'i* or *qi*, as in *qi gong*. In my work, I use it to mean the life force that connects us and influences everything we do. My ki (pronounced "key") can expand or contract, depending on the circumstances and my conscious intention. When I walk into a room, my ki influences that room, just as my ki is influenced by the people in it. We're always giving and receiving ki. Practicing aikido off the mat means I'm aware and purposeful in my giving and receiving.

ఴ **Dojo:** The dojo is where we practice aikido; it is the space where we get on the mat and learn aikido techniques. This can be a literal dojo (a school or studio such as our Portsmouth Aikido dojo) or a metaphorical dojo (such as a coaching session).

ఴ **Attack:** Because aikido is a martial art, I use what one colleague describes as "fighting language." Because of some of the images we see, hear, experience, and turn away from in our often adversarial culture, words such as attack, opponent, adversary, and power are laden with connotations and weight. For me, however, the word *attack* is fairly neutral—it simply describes energy coming toward me. On the mat, this can be a physical attack in the form of a grab or strike. Off the mat, when I use the word, it may include harsh feedback, demeaning language, or a difficult person or attitude, but not a physical attack.

ఴ **Centered presence:** When I'm centered and present, I am confident, flexible, focused, calm, and prepared for any eventuality. My conflict buttons can't be pushed; they are removed when I'm centered. Instead, I'm connected to something bigger: my personal power and life purpose. *Mindfulness* is another way to describe this mind-body state, and aikido is just one way of finding it.

ఴ **Purpose:** I use the word *purpose* intentionally and in similar ways throughout the book. In my life and work, I find that clarity of purpose is instrumental to the effective resolution of any conflict and an essential element for accomplishing anything of importance, such as holding a difficult conversation, cultivating a relationship, or creating a life. Purpose is the first strategy on the 6-Step Checklist in Chapter 5. Each component of our four-phase process begins with a Primary Purpose. And, as you will see, an individual's ability to clarify their purpose for entering this process is a contributing factor in its successful completion.

I'll explain other words and phrases as we go along.

As with any other metaphor, aikido words and phrases help us understand our stories about conflict in ways that are different and unfamiliar, allowing us to step out of our story and see our patterns and habitual reactions anew. Stepping back lets us see more clearly.

Aikido is also:

- ☙ A visual and kinesthetic expression of moving off a point of view in order to see another—a best-practice concept found throughout conflict resolution theory and practice.

- ☙ A demonstration of how to remain simultaneously powerful and flexible when faced with difficulty—a foundational life skill.

- ☙ A different way to view conflict—as something to be embraced and utilized for the benefit of all involved.

Aikido Is a Practical Tool

Over the years, the practice of aikido became for me a practical tool for both physical self-defense and managing everyday conflict—the clashes of personalities, ideas, goals, roles, and worldviews we experience at work and at home. Along the way, the daily repetition of physical technique embedded aikido principles into my very cells. While it's true that conflict still exists in my life (just ask my family and friends), the aikido metaphor makes it easier to address. Adversaries become partners in problem-solving. Contests of will appear as opportunities to find common ground. And the energy of attack is just a gift in disguise.

Although the idea of aikido may seem exotic or unduly daunting, you are practicing aikido whenever you listen with curiosity to an opposing view, or search for mutual understanding, respect, and purpose. Aikido happens any time you stop, take a breath, and choose a centered state of being. No matter how you approach it, whether physically or conceptually, aikido offers a unique blend of power and grace. In life, the aikido metaphor is realized when you sense the learning opportunity in conflict and adapt to new circumstances with ease, moving with life's flow instead of struggling against it.

Whether I'm presenting workshops, coaching, or writing, this martial art permeates my thinking and teaching. I offer "Aikido Off the Mat" lessons throughout the book to broaden your understanding of the martial art as well as the work you and your employees are doing, and to have some fun. As we go along, you'll learn how the aikido lens can be useful in every corner of life without ever physically getting on the mat.

The Four Phases

This book is organized in phases, similar to how aikido is practiced as a martial art. On the mat, I:

1. **Bow in.** I bow in to the space with respect and gratitude for what I'll learn there, bringing myself fully into my surroundings and knowing that my intention will affect my practice.

2. **Enter and blend.** I acquire techniques to enter and blend with each opponent's energy, for the purpose of aligning, joining, and harnessing that energy rather than resisting it.

3. **Redirect.** I learn to redirect my opponent's energy toward a peaceful and sustainable resolution to the conflict. I turn an enemy into an ally.

4. **Bow out.** I bow out at the end, offering thanks to my partners and teachers, knowing there is more to learn.

The four phases comprise a practical handbook for addressing the questions leaders may have when employees vital to the organization don't get along:

ↈ "Should I intervene?"

ↈ "Do I bring them together or work with them individually?"

  ❧ "What do I say?"

  ❧ "How do I ensure cooperation and positive results?"

  ❧ "What tools, skills, and practices will help me?"

The phases and chapters help you organize your intervention. You can follow them in the order I offer here or start where you feel most comfortable. The phases merge and overlap, and that's okay. That's the way conflict resolution happens: You move with the energy in the room.

When I write about measuring the parties' abilities in Chapter 3, for example, I'm also inviting you to think about skill development, which is the focus of later chapters. To teach communication effectiveness, you need skills in emotion management and centered presence. To make these skills easy to absorb, I outline them in separate chapters (Chapters 4 and 5) when in reality, they aren't separate at all. The first phase, Work on Yourself Alone, is an ongoing directive that permeates every phase and chapter.

We look at ways you can implement each step in your workplace. And, there's a handy quick-reference guide at the end of the book. Each phase has a specific focus.

Phase 1: Bowing In

In Chapter 1, you build your personal competency and mindset for reframing conflict as opportunity—the understanding that conflict is real and inevitable, and that its energy can be an opening to learn, grow, and change if we see the possibilities it offers.

You'll learn how, as an individual and facilitator of the process, your attitude toward what's happening in a conflict makes all the difference. You'll also identify the conflict management skills and centered presence to help you be effective and purposeful in working with the conflicting parties. This chapter is the key to increasing your leadership presence, resilience, and ability to manage the unexpected—assets that make everything about your job easier and more satisfying.

Because the concept of a learning mindset is integral to conflict resolution and an extension of centered presence, it is developed further in Chapter 4, where you'll find activities to reinforce this learning mindset with the people you're coaching.

Phase 2: Entering and Blending (Individual Sessions)

Phase 2 is your entry into the conflict. My experience is that it's important not to bring the parties together at first, but to meet with them individually for a few sessions to understand the conflict from both viewpoints and to see what each person wants and needs in order to move forward. Chapter 2 offers overarching themes and helpful behaviors for these individual sessions. The goal is for the parties to have time and space to tell their version of the conflict story as well as how it is affecting them and their work.

During the individual sessions, the parties also begin to gain appreciation for their conflict partner's side of things and prepare to enter the next phase of setting their differences aside.

In Chapter 3, you determine if the parties are committed to the process, help them find their motivation, and develop an alternate plan if they're unwilling or unable to move forward.

Once you know you have willing participants, Chapters 4 and 5 focus on the core of the model: building awareness and skills in centered presence, emotion management, purposeful communication, and problem-solving.

Phase 3: Redirecting (Joint Sessions)

When you're ready to bring the parties together, Phase 3 shows you how to start and follow the process to a successful resolution.

Chapter 6 offers ways to make sure the first joint session is a success. In Chapter 7, you find topics and questions that build rapport, keep conversations flowing, and smoothly broach areas of the conflict that are ready to be resolved. In addition, you see how to stimulate further conversation about people's values, new wisdom gained, and what a sustainable resolution looks like.

If you decide to document and catalog the sessions' accomplishments in a final letter of agreement, Chapter 8 offers tips for doing so.

Phase 4: Bowing Out

In the aikido metaphor, the coaching sessions represent the mat, and our conflict parties are "on the mat" in the sense that they're learning and practicing techniques to manage conflict as individuals and in relationships. The parties are learning to "dance" together in a new, more cooperative way.

Life and work being what they are, when the process ends, people are often tempted to fall into old patterns. It's important that the parties leave with agreements, written or otherwise, about how to follow up and continue working with each other. This last phase of our process takes the practice off the mat and into the workplace.

When the coaching process is finished and the pressure returns, the parties need ways to manage the emotions that inevitably recur. Chapter 8 is about fostering accountability and continuing to build the relationship by exploring future challenges and planning follow-up reinforcement.

Getting on the Mat

I include many examples to illustrate the book's focus. Each scenario comes from an actual facilitation in my work with clients. Names and aspects of the narratives have been changed, but the process is representative of what occurred, demonstrating how each part of the intervention played out.

Each chapter describes a component of the intervention (Primary Purpose, Preparation, and Agenda) and detailed coaching instructions.

With this in mind, I hope you're ready to jump in. You can use the book in various ways, depending on your goals and needs. For example, you can:

- Start with Phase 1 and read the entire book.

- Review the Purpose, Preparation, and Agenda at the beginning of each chapter.

- Skim the end-of-chapter summaries, or go directly to the quick-reference guide at the end of the book, where I offer a "lite" version of the four-phase process.

- ∽ Jump to specific chapters that will help you address an urgent situation.

- ∽ Use the book to refresh, reinforce, and expand your already existing skill set by looking at it through the aikido lens.

Whatever approach you choose, you'll soon be on the path to resolving workplace conflict as well as creating more peace and productivity. This approach is founded on the premise that you can help resolve employee conflict with conscious intention and some key skills, which are translatable and transferable. This represents an investment of time and energy, and it is worthwhile work. Your willingness to begin, this book, and the resources it provides combine to offer a path to positive improvement in your people and your workplace.

Are you ready for things to change?

Sources

- ∽ "A Startling 98% of Managers Feel Managers Need More Training," Victor Lipman

- ∽ "Workplace Conflict and How Businesses Can Harness It to Thrive," CPP, Inc.

- ∽ Thomas F. Crum Associates, *http://ThomasCrum.com*

- ∽ "Resolving Conflict in the Workplace—HR Survey Results," *https://www.mediation4.co.uk*

PHASE 1
BOWING IN

Your goal is to use yourself intentionally as an instrument of influence in the process.

1 WORK ON YOURSELF ALONE

With life comes conflict. We must learn to joyfully dance on a shifting carpet.
—Thomas Crum, *The Magic of Conflict*

Primary Purpose

Working on yourself is ongoing, foundational, and critical to maintaining the presence, power, and purpose required of you as you help your employees regain balance and centered presence with each other. In this phase, you determine your motivation for learning how to facilitate conflicts on your team, knowing that your intention and clarity are important to the success of the intervention. You also develop and maintain a positive mindset and learning orientation toward what is to follow.

Preparation

Consider your purpose for beginning the intervention. Refer to Appendix A, "Before Action Review," on pages 167–168 for help with this step.

- Clarify your desired outcomes for each individual, yourself, and the organization.
- Be aware of your assumptions, judgments, and concerns.
- Be open to surprises.
- Enter with optimism for a positive outcome.

Agenda

- ✣ A Positive Mindset
- ✣ Centered Presence
- ✣ Personal Power
- ✣ Clarity of Purpose
- ✣ Practices and Attitudes to Maximize Presence, Power, and Purpose
- ✣ Practices and Attitudes Detrimental to the Process
- ✣ Before You Engage
- ✣ Understand the Process

I was hired by a multidisciplinary healthcare practice to help three physicians resolve an organizational conflict. Because of his reputation as a dominating, perfectionistic figure, I entered my first meeting with Douglas, the lead physician, with some trepidation. The purpose of this session was to show Douglas the results of the 360-Degree Conflict Dynamics Profile he had recently completed.

To make sure I was prepared, I studied the results of his profile carefully and thought through how I would present the data, some of which I was fairly sure he would not agree with or want to hear. Working on myself alone, I also took a moment to envision a productive session, reminding myself to center periodically, keep a positive mindset, and be prepared for anything. Sure enough, I arrived at our scheduled time and ended up waiting forty minutes before Douglas called me in.

I said hello. Douglas did not reply. In his office, there was a desk and one chair—his. A couch stood perpendicular to and across the room from the desk. As he sat down, he directed his body toward the desk and away from me. I asked if we could sit so he could see the materials. He waved his hand, indicating that things were fine as they were.

This fascinating beginning seemed filled with breeches of professional courtesy. Here I was, asked to make a presentation to someone who seemed only remotely interested in the content. By his conscious or unconscious design, his behavior communicated that he held the power, that my report and I were meaningless intrusions on a busy day, and that the sooner this was over, the sooner he could get back to important items on his agenda.

I realized that to do the job for which I was hired, I had to take charge of the environment in a more purposeful way. I took a conscious breath and thought about aikido and how I might align with Douglas's energy.

I stated what I thought I was there to do and asked if he saw things in a similar way. (Yes, he did. Excellent.) I explained that it was important for him to be able to see the data in the report and follow along. I opened the door to his office, found a chair in the hall, carried it over to his desk, and positioned it so we were now side by side.

Next, I invited his energy with open-ended questions. What did he think was the purpose for our session? What would be his ideal outcome? Which parts of the instrument interested him most?

Gradually, by remaining centered, curious, nonjudgmental, and true to purpose, I began to redirect Douglas toward being my ally in attempting to solve a problem. Little by little, Douglas joined me in that endeavor. He saw I was not there to expose or criticize, but to support him.

It was a valuable learning experience in the ways we can shape relationships by the way we show up.

A Positive Mindset

No one learns as much about a subject as one who is forced to teach it.
— Peter F. Drucker

Research shows that a manager's attitude toward a conflict is crucial to how the impasse is resolved. In 2016, the *International Journal of Conflict Management* cited an Australian study of 401 employees in sixty-nine work groups. The study was designed to investigate what happens when a third-party supervisor intervenes to help manage a conflict. In cases where employees had a supervisor with a positive conflict-management style (CMS) the result was reduced anxiety, depression, and bullying. In addition, researchers discovered a strong connection between a positive CMS and a decrease in the number of times employees thought about filing a workers' compensation claim.

Especially in situations with a lot of history and high emotion, before you can successfully guide others through a conflict, you must first examine your own attitude, emotions, and beliefs around what is possible and understand what your role is in bringing out those possibilities.

I call this way of self-reflecting "working on yourself alone," a concept from the writings of Arnold and Amy Mindell, founders of the Process Work approach to resolving conflict.

"Working on myself alone" means observing the mindset with which I come into the process of resolving a conflict. For example, what judgments might I have made about Douglas when I first entered the room with him? I could have seen him as trying to diminish me and devalue my attempts at support. Instead, I changed my mindset to appreciate his unfamiliarity with this process, which increased my ability to redirect his behavior by helping him understand the process.

As you begin to work with your employees, are you looking forward to supporting them? What judgments are you making? What is your attitude toward each one?

The skill- and rapport-building sessions that you conduct with the parties involved in the conflict offer continuous opportunities to notice your beliefs, assumptions, and emotions. Who you are and how you choose to be present with the parties help determine the success of the endeavor. Your goal is to use yourself intentionally as an instrument of influence in the process. If you become uncentered at any point—for example, by losing your composure or becoming emotionally triggered—it's important that you find your way back. By training yourself to notice your own anger, judgment, blame, and premature conclusions, you can learn to let them go and return to supporting the parties and the process.

Knowing about the ways in which my presence can affect the process, I continually cultivate an awareness of my own physical and mental behavior as I lead an intervention. By lead, I don't mean control. I ask honest, open-ended questions, listen nonjudgmentally, stay centered and curious, and always keep purpose in mind. I smile a lot. I work to minimize nervousness, fear, and judgment in the room, and I find things I like and appreciate in each of the parties.

My posture, demeanor, eye contact, and even the way I walk into the room speak volumes. As I learned with Douglas, my belief in whether this is a learning experience with a positive outcome or a situation fraught with challenge is communicated before I say a word. Consequently, I look for positive benefits and believe in the learning that will take place. I can't pretend. I have to truly believe the intervention benefits the parties involved and that I am a supportive factor in facilitating the resolution of the conflict. My mindset is a principal ally throughout this process, as it is in life.

Mirror Neurons

In the last part of the twentieth century, scientists discovered neurons in the human brain that mimic the actions and emotions of those around us. For example, when one person's face reflects frustration, the neurons identified with those facial movements also fire in an observer's brain, eliciting similar emotions. For this reason, these neurons were named "mirror neurons." In the Harvard Business Review's *"Social Intelligence and the Biology of Leadership," Daniel Goleman and Richard Boyatzis write: "When we consciously or unconsciously detect someone else's emotions through their actions, our mirror neurons reproduce those emotions. Collectively, these neurons create an instant sense of shared experience."*

In one of the more amazing studies referenced by Goleman and Boyatzis, a group of employees received positive feedback from a leader who exhibited negative emotions (narrowed eyes, frowning) during the feedback session. Even though the feedback was positive, these employees reported feeling worse about their performance than employees who received negative feedback given with a positive affect (head nodding, smiles).

Clearly, the way in which the message is delivered has more impact than the message itself.

Presence, Power, and Purpose

As you work on yourself alone, there are three nonverbal qualities you bring with you at every phase of the process:

1. Your centered presence

2. Your personal power

3. Your clarity of purpose

As we go forward, these three qualities help you manage your mindset and behavior. They are your guides when questions arise and decisions are made. When you feel you've lost your way, let these qualities bring you back to where you need to be. The steps in this process are not as important as how you enact the steps, and my practice in aikido informs how I understand and embody these qualities.

Centered Presence

Underlying and connecting all aspects of the aikido-conflict metaphor is the ability to direct our life energy consciously and intentionally. Call it what you will—self-control, composure, mindfulness—your ability to manage *you* is where it all begins. On the aikido mat, when the attack comes, we learn to "center and extend ki." (Remember: *Ki* is the Japanese word for "energy" or "universal life force.") To be centered in this sense means to be balanced, calm, and connected to an inner source of power. In life as in aikido, when you're centered, you are more effective, capable, and in control.

When you center and extend ki, you increase your ability to influence your environment and your relationships. An awareness of how you are managing your energy is vital in helping others manage conflict.

Personal Power

In your role as manager, parent, partner, or workmate, have you noticed how you influence a conversation by your presence in it? We are always influencing because we're always giving and receiving energy. When you enter the room, the energy in that room changes. The more intentional you can be with your energy—by purposefully extending your ki—the more influence you have in the outcome of events. In other words, by observing and drawing on your personal power—your ki—you enhance your ability to bring about your stated purpose.

Aikido Off the Mat: Personal Power and Intentionality

As you coach your conflicted employees, apply your growing awareness of centered presence and personal power as follows.

Before each session, whether individual or joint, do a mental assessment: Are you worried things will go badly, or are you planning for them to go well?

Your primary job is to believe with confidence that the outcome is not predetermined, and that the conflict is actually potential energy you and your employees can harness toward a positive result. This is where your power lies.

More than likely, the employee is nervous and worried. If you enter the session with fear, judgment, or tension, you're setting the stage for an unhappy outcome. If, on the other hand, you approach the conversation with an optimistic, hopeful mindset, you foster more of the same. When you offer assurances that the individual can benefit from the process and be able to make the necessary changes, you encourage trust.

If you don't have this positive mindset, you must reexamine your purpose and work on yourself to find the mindset you need. Or, alternatively, you can call on another party to manage the intervention.

Clarity of Purpose

As you move toward intervention, consider your purpose for doing so. Some purposes are more useful than others. From the following list, choose the ones you think are useful and the ones you think might not be.

       ✿ Help the parties learn that conflict can lead to greater understanding of each other as well as a more productive and positive workplace.

    ☙ Make sure these people get over their difficulty and stop acting out.

    ☙ Change the relationship in any way I can.

    ☙ Help the parties see and maximize what they have in common as well as leverage their differences.

    ☙ Get through this situation as quickly as possible.

You may laugh at some of these examples, but purposes can be hidden. For example, I may think my purpose is to communicate a difference of opinion, but hidden in the background is an intention to make sure you know how angry I am. Or I may say I want to help the parties use the conflict to learn about each other and create a more positive workplace, but my actions say I just want to get through this and move on to more important things.

What do you really want for yourself, the parties involved, and the organization? What is your highest and best purpose? Continually clarify your purpose, and keep it at the forefront of each session you conduct.

Practices and Attitudes to Maximize Presence, Power, and Purpose

Bringing the three qualities of centered presence, personal power, and clarity of purpose to a conflict situation is easier said than done. Conflict usually robs us of all three, as we struggle to do the right thing, find the perfect answer, and maintain psychological safety and equilibrium.

Fortunately, conflict can also provide the perfect crucible to practice bringing these vital qualities to any situation. On the following pages, I discuss ways of acting and being that I've discovered add to my power and presence as well as help me return to purpose when things get difficult.

1. Reframing

In aikido, it's often said that the opponent's attack is a gift of energy. At first glance, it is difficult to imagine conflict or aggression as a gift. In many cases, I would rather not have to deal with a problem. Nevertheless, it is present and taking up mental space. The question becomes: Should I waste valuable life energy (ki) wishing it away, or should I turn it into a positive force?

After many years of practicing and teaching aikido, and applying its principles in the workplace, I've found that things change dramatically when I reframe an attack as incoming energy that can be guided toward a mutually supportive outcome. In aikido, my goal is to keep myself safe while supporting my opponent-partner. Regardless of my partner's intention, mine is clear: I intend to disarm without harming and guide the energy toward a mutual purpose (the key word here is "mutual"). Enter, blend, and redirect. The spirit in which the coaching is entered into makes a huge difference.

When dealing with your employee conflict, you can use the conflict energy to reframe the problem in the following way.

This conflict is an opportunity for both parties:

- ☙ To change their relationship for the better.

- ☙ To learn valuable work and life skills.

- ☙ To see each other's positive aspects.

- ☙ To step into leadership roles and model conflict competency in the organization.

- ☙ To solve problems together using their differences as assets.

All of these statements could also be useful purposes for your intervention.

2. Possibility

When coaching people in conflict, I ask what possibilities exist for each of the participants as well as how the resolution affects the larger team and organization. Although you may be working with just two people, a positive change in their relationship can create constructive waves throughout the system. For example, dialogue may flow more freely between all team members when the logjam of this particular relationship is cleared. Time and energy previously claimed by the conflict is released and freed up for the people and processes that need them.

It's the coach's role to help everyone see how a positive outcome liberates untapped potential—for the parties in the conflict and for others. Wherever possible, I recommend documenting drained resources, reduced momentum, and other hidden or indirect costs that are likely to improve when the conflict is resolved.

When John joined Taylor's department in their company's regional production center, they somehow got off on the wrong foot. Their work stalled, productivity suffered, and their teammates first avoided the conflict then polarized around it.

I worked with John and Taylor individually for three months, helping them to build skills and see each other differently. Then, the three of us held several joint sessions. We discussed behaviors that had caused difficulty, and worked through how John and Taylor would manage their interactions going forward. Last, we brought the rest of the team into the conversation by being transparent about the process and inviting them to support John and Taylor in their new relationship.

When I later followed up with the manager, she reported that teamwork became more relaxed, easy, and open as the men freed themselves from the conflict that had immobilized everyone.

---

3. Non-Judgment

When you coach, if at any point you start to draw conclusions about which party is right and which is wrong, it becomes difficult to do your job effectively. If you judge one of the parties as the problem, it will be hard for you to see their positive intent. And you may miss constructive actions or recast neutral behaviors in unhelpful ways.

As human beings, we are practiced at forming judgments about everything, and we're usually unaware we're doing it. For example, if I have a workshop to give and there's a blizzard raging, I automatically judge this as a bad thing. When I make this assessment, my body tenses, my mood deteriorates, and I become angry. This doesn't change the weather—it is what it is. I still have to decide what action to take. Do I cancel the workshop or continue as planned? Seeing the weather as a neutral event reduces my stress level, saves time, and improves my ability to make a wise decision.

Aikido Off the Mat: The Practice of Non-Judgment

As you work on yourself alone, you can apply the aikido principles of entering, blending, and redirecting to the practice of nonjudgment with increasing inner awareness.

The first step is to enter—to notice that you're judging and witness your judging mind at work. Then blend or align with the judgment; determine if it's accurate, helpful, or useful. Regardless of its accuracy, judgment hampers your ability to facilitate the process. Instead, redirect your mind toward curiosity and openness. Think about what skills each party needs and how they can attain them.

The power of non-judgment becomes clear when you see others changed by it. As they learn non-judgment from you, the individuals in a coaching process become more open to each other and more willing to entertain each other's positive intent. People begin to see themselves and others as more generous, kind, and forgiving.

I have a colleague who models non-judgment extremely well. She's a great listener who seldom offers advice, instead preferring to ask questions that promote reflection. In one case, she was coaching two women who had been workplace adversaries for a long time. With my colleague's help, they eventually found a new way to interact. A few weeks after the coaching process ended, one of the women reported back to my colleague: "I don't know what you did to us, but I've hated her for ten years, and I actually like her now."

What my colleague did was to listen without judgment until two women felt fully heard. The power of non-judgment is tangible and communicable.

4. Curiosity and Inquiry

More than anything else, a mindset of curiosity and inquiry empowers you and keeps your conversations safe and on track. When the atmosphere in an intervention becomes charged with emotion, I practice using the aikido principles of entering, blending, and redirecting by asking open-ended questions, such as:

- "How did you feel when that happened?"
- "What were you hoping for?"
- "What do you think your coworker's intention was?"
- "What was your intention?"

A previous client of mine—while technically savvy and an outstanding leader in a Fortune 100 company—found it difficult to practice curiosity and was easily triggered by behavior she considered irritating. In one session, we talked about a colleague's email etiquette. The colleague's penchant for copying a long list of people on every email angered my client, particularly when the email reflected poorly on the department. During one practice session, I asked the client to devise questions she could ask her colleague to understand the intent behind copying so many people. One question she came up with was, "Why did you copy everyone on that email?"

The content of the question was fine, but as we role-played asking it, my client sounded confrontational. I asked if she noticed the tone of her delivery (she did) and what would have to change for her to ask the question in an open, curious way. She answered, smiling, "I'd actually have to be curious." We both laughed as she absorbed the "aha moment." It's not what we say, but whether we're curious or judging when we say it.

When you feel judgmental, shift your mindset. Get curious. Ponder. Wonder. The more you practice this important skill, the more you'll learn about each person's perspective. And the more you model it for others, the more you encourage their curiosity.

5. Appreciation

Appreciative Inquiry is another example of aikido in the workplace, one that maximizes the power of noticing what is already working rather than focusing on what is broken. Since David Cooperrider introduced the concept in 1987, organizations and individuals have been using Appreciative Inquiry to solve problems and imagine what could be. Practitioners have learned that as soon as you align with the positive, you gain energy and move toward a compelling future.

A concrete example of Appreciative Inquiry happens every time a beginner learns a new technique on the aikido mat. Invariably, the new technique is easier to do on one side of the body than the other. Instead of trying to fix the "bad" side, the instructor tells the student to focus on the "good" side (the side that can do the technique effortlessly). Since that side knows how to do it, aikido instructors say to "let the good side teach the other side."

In my coaching interventions, I encourage people to appreciate what's positive and learn from it. For example, when coaching Douglas and his colleagues at their health-care practice, I learned there were often times when the team collaborated without conflict. I inquired what it was about these situations that allowed the team to work together harmoniously. At first they weren't sure, but with some reflection, it came to light that when things flowed more easily, the teammates were clear on their roles and the purpose for the endeavor. Ah! Clarity of roles and goals! We began to investigate how the team could be clearer about roles and goals in other situations.

When you help your employees focus on the good, you reinforce their strengths, knowledge, and positive attributes. When they find the areas in which they work well together, coworkers can apply that awareness to areas in which they have difficulty. Setbacks, too, are part of the process and teach us what needs to happen next. Throughout the coaching, whether you're reinforcing strengths or acknowledging a challenging setback, you can appreciate the employees' commitment as they build a new relationship and a foundation for solving future problems.

Practices and Attitudes that Are Detrimental to the Process

Harried, overworked, and overwhelmed as we are, we often experience our students, patients, clients, colleagues, and children as difficult, irresponsible, rude, dull, or simply too numerous to keep track of. But if we mean to choose the world, we must see God in the people who come under our care. That is, we must see them as at bottom no different from ourselves.
—Philip Simmons, *Learning to Fall*

Just as certain practices and mindsets promote success in managing conflict, others can derail the process. Have you ever found yourself uttering the following phrases—or thinking them? I know I have. Consider the phrases and their antidotes.

This is not my job.

This is exactly your job. As a supervisor, manager, owner, or CEO, you are a leader—and leaders lead. You show the way. You model. You put forth a vision and invite others to join in.

This is why it's vital to manage your attitude for maximum power and presence, and to keep your purpose in mind. If you don't feel ready to lead in this way, consider calling in someone else you believe is right for the job.

I don't have the skills to do this.

This may be true. If so, this is a great opportunity for you to learn the skills to become a more effective, respected, and responsible manager. Through your learning, you will increase trust and build influence with your team.

This will take too much time.

Even when you know the importance of actively addressing workplace conflict, you may wonder where to find the time. Ask yourself:

    ◦◦ How much is the conflict costing in wasted hours, lost or unhappy staff and/or customers, and stifled creativity?

    ◦◦ Are you waking up at night wondering what to do?

    ◦◦ Do you avoid certain meetings because of the conflict?

    ◦◦ Is the tension affecting others?

    ◦◦ Does the conflict limit the team's ability to accomplish goals?

Whatever time the process takes will be less than the time you, your customers, and your company lose in reduced productivity and goodwill. In my experience, it takes more time *not* to resolve conflict than to address it.

They should just rise above it.

I've heard this phrase too many times to count; your staff would if they could.

I recently conducted a series of coaching sessions with two employees of a food manufacturing company. As I met with the employees individually, they each told me that when they asked their manager for help, he suggested they "just rise above it." They said they tried, but they didn't know how. Just being in each other's presence was enough to shut down conversation and workflow.

If your employees could make wiser choices, they would. It helps the process immeasurably when you believe your employees are doing the best they can with the skills they have and help them acquire the skills they currently lack.

What's wrong with these people?!

Ask instead: "What do they need to help them through this?" "What are they blind to?" "How can I help them see what they're missing?"

They're mean, disrespectful, and hurtful.

They're unskilled.

When you reframe negative intent as a need for skill-building, you shift from judge to coach. You also see what the people in conflict really want (recognition, support, autonomy, and inclusion) and how their (sometimes misguided) attempts to achieve these goals have an unexpected, negative impact. Being able to reframe the situation also means you can help your team get where they want to go more effectively.

> *In the aikido school I founded, Sam practiced with us for a number of years. In the beginning, no one liked seeing him in class. He usually came in late, during pre-class meditation time, when the rest of us were sitting quietly on the mat. Sam would enter, drop his large key ring noisily on a chair, sigh or make some other attention-grabbing sound, and after much ado, finally bow onto the mat and join us. Another of Sam's regrettable habits was to insinuate his way into private conversations. He was not well liked, and yet he came to every class and seemed committed to learning aikido.*
>
> *I let things go for a while, not knowing what to do ("This is not my job!") and harboring my own judgments about Sam ("What's wrong with this person?! He's so disrespectful!").*
>
> *In time, I realized it was my job. I was the chief instructor and owner of the school. If I didn't address this difficult situation, the class environment would deteriorate. I also changed my story about Sam. Instead of seeing only a disruptive influence, I imagined a more positive intention. Maybe he was seeking attention and just wanted to fit in. So I gave Sam some attention in the form of a brief conversation after class one day. I explained the impact of his behavior on the other students, while also appreciating his commitment to learning aikido. He took it well, and told me he had no idea he was so noisy and didn't mean to be disrespectful. He only wanted to make new friends. Unfortunately, he was going about it in all the wrong ways, leaving a wide gap between intent and impact. After our conversation, he made an effort to fit in differently, and his relationships improved.*

Before You Engage

To give yourself the best chance at success as you begin to engage with the parties in conflict, answer the following questions. Continually hold them in your awareness for each session, but especially for the initial meeting.

What is the purpose of the intervention? What do I really want—for each individual, for the relationship, and for the organization?

Imagine the ideal outcome for the intervention, and the ease and flow of each day once this difficulty has been resolved. How will the individuals interact, and how will the team and organization reflect the shift? The clearer and more detailed the vision, the more likely it will come to be.

Am I contributing to the problem?

Your actions may have unknowingly helped the situation develop. For example, have you avoided talking with the parties? Have you fallen victim to one or more of the detrimental attitudes listed earlier in this section? It's only human nature to hope people will "rise above it," to think you "don't have the skills," or to worry this course of action will take "too much time."

Once you determine your contribution to the conflict, you can more clearly see how you can help resolve it.

What actions have I already taken that have helped or hindered?

Review the conversations you've had with each party prior to the session. What went well? Looking forward, what will you do differently?

What is the best alternative to a successful resolution of the conflict?

If the parties are unable to reach an amicable way to work together and take their relationship to the next level, what is Plan B? How will you implement it? Is this alternative something you will share with the participants or hold in reserve?

Understand the Process

What you're about to undertake is a process of coaching, facilitation, and conflict resolution. It requires time, energy, and commitment.

Your greatest asset is the quality of your being: centered presence, personal power, and clarity of purpose. Everything else is secondary. Your influence originates in your attitude, thoughts, posture, and breath. When you pause for reflection, so does everyone else. When you shift from certainty to curiosity—and from judgment to appreciation—others also relax and become more centered. The change in energy is palpable and profound.

If you believe in the process and your people, you will lead them to a satisfying conclusion.

Key Points

∾ Working on yourself is ongoing and foundational for you to help your employees come to center.

∾ Centered presence, personal power, and clarity of purpose are integral to every phase of the conflict resolution process.

∾ Underlying and connecting all aspects of the aikido-conflict metaphor is the ability to direct your life energy in a conscious and purposeful way.

∾ It is necessary to clarify your purpose for the intervention and to keep this purpose at the forefront of each session.

∾ Certain attitudes maximize presence, power, and purpose. Conversely, there are attitudes that are detrimental to the process.

Sources

∾ "Social Intelligence and the Biology of Leadership," *Harvard Business Review, https://hbr.org*

∾ Arnold Mindell, *http://www.aamindell.net*

∾ Wendy Palmer, *http://www.embodimentinternational.com*

∾ Morihei Ueshiba, *https://en.wikipedia.org/wiki/Morihei_Ueshiba*

∾ Aikido Master Morihei Ueshiba: "Highlights of 'Takemusu Aiki," *https://www.youtube.com/watch?v=8V7NHLlmT3Y*

∾ "O Sensei Morihei Ueshiba," *https://www.youtube.com/watch?v=XoDK3XuvZWw*

∾ Portsmouth Aikido, *https://www.portsmouthaikido.org*

∾ Power & Presence Training, *www.judyringer.com*

∾ David Cooperrider/Appreciative Inquiry, *http://www.davidcooperrider.com*

∾ Kirsten A. Way, Nerina L. Jimmieson, Prashant Bordia, "Shared Perceptions of Supervisor Conflict Management Style: A Cross-Level Moderator of Relationship Conflict and Employee Outcomes," *International Journal of Conflict Management*, 27 no. 1 (2014): 25–49; doi.org/10.1108/IJCMA-07-2014-0046

As a coach, it's important to curb your well-intentioned impulse to solve the problem.

One of the simplest ways to practice the alignment of aikido is to listen with interest to people's stories.

2 ALIGN AND ENGAGE

The heart of most conflict is not irreconcilable differences, but irreconcilable stories.
—Joseph Grenny, *Crucial Conversatsions*

Primary Purpose

Chapter 2 is an overview of how to approach all the individual sessions, regardless of how many sessions are required. The primary purpose of Chapter 2 is to equip you with tools to hear and validate each party's distinct narrative of the conflict.

Chapter 3 specifically addresses what happens in the first individual session.

Chapters 4 and 5 contain conflict and communication practices you can use to coach the parties in the individual sessions.

Preparation

- ✐ Know the purpose and desired outcome for each session.
- ✐ Review your notes.
- ✐ Enter with optimism for a positive outcome.

Agenda

- ✐ Ask for any new developments since the last session.
- ✐ Discuss ways to prepare for the next session and set a date.

ᢙ Take notes; send them in a follow-up email after each session.

ᢙ Assign homework.

Homework

To fully engage the parties in the process, I've found it helpful to give homework assignments that reinforce the focus of each session and prepare them for the next. At the end of most chapters, I give examples of homework, such as reading, self-reflection, and experiential activities. I also list additional books, articles, and websites in the Further Resources section at the back of the book. The point is to support the parties and their process in as many ways as possible, and to maintain momentum between sessions.

If you want to prepare by reading some of the books in advance, I recommend the following:

ᢙ *Unlikely Teachers: Finding the Hidden Gifts in Daily Conflict* by Judy Ringer

ᢙ *Managing Conflict with Power & Presence Workbook* by Judy Ringer

ᢙ *The Magic of Conflict* by Thomas Crum

ᢙ *Journey to Center* by Thomas Crum

ᢙ *Three Deep Breaths* by Thomas Crum

ᢙ *Difficult Conversations: How to Discuss What Matters Most* by Douglas Stone, Bruce Patton, and Sheila Heen

ᢙ *Crucial Conversations: Tools for Talking When the Stakes are High* by Patterson, Grenny, McMillan, and Switzler

ᢙ *Emotional Intelligence* by Daniel Goleman

ᢙ *Thanks for the Feedback* by Douglas Stone and Sheila Heen

ᢙ *The Elephant in the Room* by Diana McLain Smith

ᢙ *Mindset* by Carol S. Dweck, PhD

ᢙ *Radical Candor* by Kim Scott

ᢙ *Triggers* by Marshall Goldsmith

ᢙ *Ask Powerful Questions* by Will Wise

Greg, the founder, and Jason, the executive director, had very different visions of how their non-profit should operate. The agency was successful, and had huge support from the population it served locally and nationally. But Greg and Jason's internal struggle was creating stress in the work environment and polarizing the workforce.

After three years of working together, Greg and Jason were growing further apart. Tensions increased as staff members were increasingly drawn into the conflict, even as they struggled to remain neutral. Greg and Jason both had stories about how things had evolved, and although each story was true for the teller, it only reinforced the separation. The truth was that the two people most invested in the organization, and important to its health and well-being, had difficulty communicating civilly.

I was there to help them rebuild their relationship so they could continue to build their organization.

We met individually for five sessions. Greg and Jason each felt a sense of relief in being able to tell their stories to someone who listened with non-judgment and empathy. I asked honest questions and acknowledged the feelings that surfaced: frustration, anger, confusion, and unhappiness that things had gone as far as they had.

I aligned with each of them in the aikido sense, in that I could see how their narrative made sense to the person telling it. I acknowledged Greg in his sessions and Jason in his. It's important to note that their feelings made sense in the context in which they experienced them, and acknowledgement was in fact what each person needed—what Jason needed to receive from Greg and what Greg needed to hear from Jason. But the nature of conflict being what it is, neither could offer that gift to the other.

This is one of the most difficult things to do in conflict—to hear and acknowledge your conflict partner's story. I do this for the parties until they can do it for each other.

Why Meet Individually?

When you have two individuals at odds—and each is valuable to the organization, knowledgeable, experienced, and compatible with everyone but each other—what do you do?

You may have tried:

ᴇ◌ **The pep talk:** "Come on, now, you can do this. Rise above it."

ᴇ◌ **The appeal to compassion and empathy:** "Try not to take things so personally; see things from his perspective."

ᴇ◌ **The common-sense approach:** "Your work is suffering. Something has to change. You don't have to be best friends, but you do have to work together and get the job done."

You may have also tried evading, ignoring, and hoping the situation would resolve itself. You've probably brought the topic up at performance reviews, and talked to colleagues, coaches, and consultants. Yet the problem persists.

Each person brings value to the organization. And they must be able to work together amicably. Consequently, you decide to keep working at the situation and bring them together to talk things through.

Although it is tempting to get everyone in the same room right away, I've learned a joint meeting at this early stage often makes matters worse. The parties don't yet have the skills or perspective they need to be open to any view but their own.

Annie, a trusted colleague and vice president of HR with a national health-care provider has had many opportunities to facilitate difficult coworker conversations during her long career. She told me she learned early on never to bring the two people together at the beginning:

I really listen to Person A. Then, I really listen to Person B. I go back and forth, meeting with the parties individually until each is ready to listen and be open to working things out.

I recall a failure early on when I was in a "hurry up and fix this" mode and didn't stick with the process I knew worked. My manager at the time told me to "just get them in a room together!" I got caught up in it and did bring them together. They were soon shouting at each other. Plus, my emotions got going and fueled the fire.

I learned from that to always meet privately first with each of the individuals and to make sure each party knows this is part of the process.

If you've already broached the problem at a joint meeting, maybe you know Annie's experience. Each individual pushes to have their perspective acknowledged. No one listens. Emotions run high. The problem escalates. This is especially true if the conflict has a long history. Each party has fine-tuned their narrative—their conflict story—about why the other person is the problem: "If only they were different, everything would be all right." At this point, the conflict may also be polarizing the work environment.

Or you may have experienced the "let's talk it out" team meeting during which one employee ends up feeling most of the heat. This can happen when, as their manager, you want to hear from all sides in the conflict. You think it will be helpful for all involved to understand each other's point of view. Plus, you hope it will save time. This kind of meeting seldom goes well, especially if you have a belief (conscious or not) that one of the people in the room is the source of the problem. Instead of resolving the conflict, one employee leaves feeling responsible, hurt, antagonistic, and unable to face the team the next day.

I like to give the parties a chance to get their feet on the ground, develop some skills, and increase their awareness of their contribution to the conflict—rather than put people in a position where they feel the need to defend themselves.

Meeting with each person individually for one or more sessions reduces defensiveness and increases the possibilities for resolution for many reasons:

    ❧ As a multi-partial third party (see sidebar on page 45), you represent what the parties cannot offer each other at this point: openness to hearing their point of view, empathy, reassurance, and acknowledgment. In other words, you provide an opportunity for each person to tell his or her story fully and without interruption.

ɛɔ Non-judgmental listening offers a release valve for the pent-up emotional energy held in each conflict story. Each person can "tell it like it is" to a willing listener.

ɛɔ Personalized instruction addresses unique needs. You match your coaching and skill building to each party's ability, and each naturally processes the coaching differently.

ɛɔ Each party learns to speak for themselves in ways that are necessary and important for the joint sessions.

Your primary task throughout the individual sessions is to ask questions, acknowledge each person's positive intent, and redirect what you hear toward a sustainable resolution. Annie calls this inquiry mode her "Columbo" method, from the television series starring Peter Falk as an unassuming homicide detective whose persistent questions gradually uncover details of the crime. Lieutenant Columbo is relentlessly curious, always delving deeper, while at the same time calmly reflecting, "Help me understand . . ." or "When you say . . . what does that mean?"

In my own practice, I take a similar approach: asking questions to discover new information, staying on the lookout for red flags, and digging deeper while remaining respectful of the process. I also practice being comfortable with silence and try to stop myself from jumping in too quickly. I wait for a few beats even after I hear an answer in case the person has more to say. I read nonverbal cues, such as someone's lack of eye contact, tears, emotional moments, or fidgeting, and I follow up on them. For example, I may ask, "Where did you go just then, when you looked away and stopped talking?" Or, "Where are the tears coming from?" I ask other questions to get at what the parties are really trying to say, such as, "When you said you don't like it when you get 'attitude' from your coworker, what does that mean? What does it look like? Can you give me a specific behavior that triggers your anger?" These kinds of questions encourage the person to say more.

It's also important to notice and challenge your assumptions. For example, you may want to believe a high performer over a more average one. Annie suggests you consider that people "may be different from your idea of who they are." Meeting with people individually gives you time to learn who each person really is, what motivates them, and the larger context for the conflict.

It's important to be truly and genuinely interested in everything about the person and their story, which creates feelings of safety, openness, and calm. The person you're meeting with understands this is not a rush job. You're completely present for the long run, not packing your bag for the next meeting.

Aikido Off the Mat: Multi-Partial vs. Neutral

I often hear clients say they want an impartial, neutral facilitator, which implies someone who is objective and able to maintain emotional distance. While impartiality and neutrality are helpful in a strategic planning session, in facilitating conflict, the ability to be multi-partial—to align with each side equally in order to fully understand it—is more useful.

At first, I was concerned that if I aligned with both sides, the parties in the conflict would think I was duplicitous. Whose side was I on? A key insight for me was realizing I could be transparent with the process, and let participants know that my job in these individual sessions is to be on their side and on their partner's side. Introducing this idea helps each party see that the situation has more than one facet. It also reinforces the idea that the "adversary" has more sides than just the part they play in the current problem. If I can appreciate the other person and understand their point of view, maybe the conflicting party can as well.

A multi-partial facilitator helps each side to tell the story. By aligning with each in turn, I redirect the emotional conflict energy so it can express itself safely and begin to defuse, bringing much-needed awareness.

Stand Side by Side

If you watch aikido closely, you'll soon observe that it's not actually fighting. The person receiving the attack doesn't block or strike back. She enters, aligns with the energy, and redirects it, keeping herself and her opponent safe. A major shift happens when you start to think this way in everyday life as well, when you begin to see an "attack" simply as an opportunity to align with incoming energy, information, or positive intent, then redirect what you receive toward a solution.

Aligning and engaging your conflict partner's energy is one of the more revolutionary aspects of aikido and is what you are doing in the individual sessions. These meetings provide an opening to stand side by side with each party in the conflict and help them redirect their fighting energy toward a more useful purpose: resolving the conflict and becoming more socially and emotionally intelligent. As we move on to the specific purpose and content for each individual session, I want to reinforce the primary instruments we use when standing side by side with each party: listening, acknowledging, and creating openings for resolution to take place.

Listen and Acknowledge

One of the most powerful methods for healing a relationship is also the simplest. It is to listen, to give one's complete attention to the aggrieved person for as long as he or she has something to say. . . . Indeed, sometimes what people really want most is a chance to have their grievance heard and acknowledged by others.
—William Ury, *Getting to Peace*

The most important thing in communication is to hear what isn't being said.
—Peter F. Drucker, management consultant and author

One of the simplest ways to practice the alignment of aikido is to listen with interest to people's stories. In the individual sessions, the players have time to relate how the conflict evolved and affects them and their work. Your job is to listen with objectivity, non-judgment, and curiosity.

Simple? Yes. But not easy. Before we move into planning the individual sessions, here are a few dos and don'ts that can help you listen.

Don't

1. **Debate.** The parties will only push back. You don't want to show them the error of their ways. They'll learn in time and through experience. Don't share what seems so obvious to you, as in "if only they could see" what you see. Your observations may be accurate, but the parties in conflict can't hear you until they have been heard. Don't store rebuttals in your mind. Instead, relax the counterarguments, and keep your mind open and focused on them. When they feel heard—whether you agree with them or not—they feel validated. They lighten. They can listen to other possible scenarios.

2. **Try to solve the problem.** It's the solution they come up with themselves that will stick. Because you're their manager, and because you can see how each person could be helped by knowing information they don't have or by benefitting from your experience, you may be tempted to offer advice, explain the larger view, tell them what they're missing, or ask leading questions. I know this because it happens every time I'm in your shoes. Your intention is positive: You want to help your people and you want to resolve the conflict. It would be so easy if they could see what you see. I also know the value of just listening without judgment, a gift that lets your employees hear themselves, and reflect on what they're thinking and saying. Solving comes later in the joint sessions, and ideally, the parties do it themselves, together.

Do

1. **Stay curious.** Curiosity is an ally that helps you maintain peace of mind. Even more than the questions you ask, the mindset of curiosity is one of the most powerful tools you have for guiding your team members' emotional energy and defusing anger. Because people appreciate the opportunity to express their emotions and clarify their intentions, curiosity has a centering effect.

2. **Ask open-ended, honest questions.** Pose questions to which you don't know the answer. Start with "what" or "how" whenever possible. Encourage the parties to get the whole story out. The following examples can help get you started:

    *   "Tell me your perspective. What's been happening?"
    *   "How did this begin?"
    *   "How does this conflict impact your work?"
    *   "What part of this problem has been most challenging?"
    *   "Tell me about a time you felt differently about . . . / got along well with . . . / worked well together? What happened to change that?"
    *   "What behaviors bother you the most?"
    *   "What behaviors are happening when things are going well?"
    *   "What is the solution from your point of view?"
    *   "How have you contributed to the conflict?"
    *   "How would (the other party) tell the story of this conflict (and answer the other questions above)?"
    *   "How do you feel about doing this conflict resolution work?"
    *   "What would an ideal partnership with this person look like?"

    Any one of these questions will get you started and, if you stay curious, will generate other questions, leading you deeper into the person's story and revealing more of their beliefs, values, and hopes—exactly what you want to happen. In Chapter 3, there are additional questions that broaden and deepen the topic at hand.

    Questions that are not useful include:

    *   "What if you tried. . . .?"
    *   "Have you thought of apologizing?"
    *   "Don't you think you're taking things too personally?"

- "How could you see things from their perspective?"
- "If I were you, I would. . . . What do you think of trying that?"

3. **Validate.** Acknowledge, clarify, and reflect back the person's view—whether you agree with it or not. For example:
   - "What I hear you saying is . . ."
   - "It makes sense you might feel that way."
   - "What you just said seems particularly important. Can you say more?"
   - "I'm sorry that happened. What about the situation was most difficult for you?"
   - "What would be an ideal solution?"

4. **Look for what they're not saying.** Notice mixed signals. The individual might say they're fine with the coaching process as outlined, for example, but you sense some hesitation. They're avoiding eye contact or reluctant to share their story. These are indications they may not be saying what's really on their mind. Continue to describe what you see and invite them to say more.

Create Openings

Your first goals are to learn and fully understand the conflict stories as well as sense the possibilities for resolution. Until the parties feel heard, they can't begin to think about moving off their positions. The more you listen, the more you offer both people the opportunity to see and hear themselves, reflect on their stories, and ponder their contributions and readiness to move toward resolution.

The individual sessions foster connection between the parties by helping them see each other differently. I often hear from managers, "These are two wonderful human beings." And you've probably had similar experiences with people in conflict who are, for you, intelligent, positive, friendly human beings. But for each other, they are difficult.

Often, contrasting learning or behavior styles can result in conflict. People have ways of operating in the world. Introversion and extraversion are two of the most common descriptors for diverging styles, and there are others. In the workplace, it's possible to perceive a divergent style as a personal attack. For example, if I'm a big-picture person, I can get irritable with a coworker who is conscientious about details. I want to move on while they're still laboring over what is, for me, a tiny point. Some people wear their "hearts on their sleeve" while others are more reserved emotionally, and may seem aloof and uncaring to a more "heart-centered" person.

When in conflict, it helps to consider that opposing styles might well be complementary strengths if employed with intention and purpose. Your attention to detail could save me from making a big mistake. My ability to see the big picture offers insight into a problem that you might not otherwise see. A behavior or personality assessment can create an opening for the parties to put their similarities and differences to good use.

By having the parties complete and (in the joint sessions) compare assessments, you gain greater perspective on your people, and they gain insight on themselves. These instruments also supply data that make for interesting conversation in the joint sessions. I usually reserve one individual session exclusively for a style instrument. The parties can complete the assessment during the session or as homework for later discussion. In the joint sessions, I ask the parties to discuss the similarities and differences in their styles, and how these differences may have contributed to their ongoing conflict.

There are a variety of instruments to choose from, some requiring training and certification. The ones I use most often are described in Appendix B starting on page 169.

The individual sessions generate opportunities for the parties to see their conflict from a wider perspective, their conflict partners as human beings with more than one facet, and themselves as potential partners in creating resolution. You and they also build skills in effective communication and conflict management.

During our five individual sessions, Greg and Jason felt their respective views of the conflict were acknowledged and were able to let go of some of their anger. They gradually grew more interested in learning how their partner's perspective differed. Each became curious about how the conflict developed and appreciative of times when the relationship was on an easier footing. Greg and Jason learned how their individual differences in style impacted their impressions of the other. The leaders saw that those differences, which often felt grating, could be huge assets if reframed as complementary strengths and redirected toward building a new working relationship—instead of seeing the differences as a problem.

In Phase 1, we explored the importance of working on yourself first—your centered presence, personal power, and clarity of purpose—in order to prepare for the intervention and the individual sessions. We also reviewed the overarching purpose for the individual sessions and how you can maximize their impact in getting the conflict resolution process off to a positive start.

In Phase 2, we look at each individual session—including frameworks, agendas, concepts, and skills—and how what comes from the individual sessions leads the process toward meeting jointly.

Key Points

- ๛ The overarching purpose for the individual sessions is to build the parties' skills, confidence, and openness to ultimately resolve the conflict in joint sessions.

- ๛ While tempting to bring the parties together right away, it is usually more productive to meet with each person individually first.

- ๛ As a multi-partial third party, you provide an opportunity for each party to tell their story fully and without interruption.

ᘓ The primary instruments you use to align with and engage the parties in resolving the conflict are: listening and acknowledging, and creating openings for resolution to take place.

ᘓ Don't debate what you hear or try to solve the problem.

ᘓ Do stay curious, ask open-ended questions, validate, and look for what the parties are not saying.

ᘓ You want to create openings for the parties to see the conflict from a wider perspective and reposition themselves as partners in creating the solution.

Phase 2
Entering and Blending
(Individual Sessions)

Helping your employees adopt the concept that conflict is neutral—and that it's up to each of us to find the gift in conflict—helps the conflict resolution process immeasurably and provides a foundational metaphor for your work.

3 MEASURE WILLINGNESS AND ABILITY

When we take responsibility for our own behavior,
we also regain control of our lives.
—Kerry Patterson, Joseph Grenny, Ron McMillan, and Al Switzler,
Crucial Conversations

Primary Purpose

In the first individual session, in which you meet with each person for the first time, your purpose is to discover whether the parties have the ability to change and are willing to commit to the process you will describe to them. Specifically, you are seeking to determine if they will try to understand the other's point of view, have an intention to resolve their differences, and commit to building a more harmonious working relationship.

Preparation

Know the purpose of the intervention. Be clear about what you want for each individual, for the relationship, and for the organization.

- ✧ Determine how you will measure each individual's commitment.

- ✧ Determine how you will measure each individual's ability to learn and change.

- ✧ Document what you already know about the parties' ability to change.

- ✧ Enter with optimism for a positive outcome.

Agenda

- ✑ Come prepared with a focus for the session.

- ✑ Express gratitude that this person agreed to meet with you to discuss the current situation.

- ✑ Build rapport.

- ✑ Explain the process you're asking them to engage in to resolve the conflict with a coworker and your role in helping them.

- ✑ Listen to their story.

- ✑ Measure their willingness.

- ✑ Estimate their ability.

- ✑ Discuss ways to prepare for the next session and set a date.

- ✑ Take notes and send them in a follow-up email after the session.

- ✑ Assign homework.

When I first met Lauren and Susan, they had been in conflict for more than two years. The presence of one was enough to trigger feelings of anger and frustration in the other. Although they initially had an easy working relationship, it deteriorated quickly due to style differences, and as their interpersonal dynamics worsened, their view of the other went from irritation to obstacle, and finally, the enemy. But they had this in common: They were each extremely skeptical of the process. During their first individual coaching sessions, they each told me they believed there was no way things could change for the better.

Everything I do serves the goal of partnering and aligning with the people I work with. For example, I talked with Lauren and Susan separately by phone to briefly explain the process and set up times when I could meet with each one individually. In each case, I arrived first and arranged the room so we were seated either side by side or at the corner of a table and not across from each other. At the start of the session, I smiled, shook hands, and showed each person I was genuinely happy to see her. I could sense each woman's hesitation and frustration about engaging in this process as well as her anxiety about being asked to move beyond her comfort zone. I set about putting each at ease with an open, positive demeanor. I wanted each to feel I was at their disposal and all would be well.

At my meeting with each woman, I described the process more fully, answered questions, and shared how she and I would work together. I explained we would meet by ourselves for a few sessions, and eventually all three of us would come together to plan how they would work together in the future. I assured each woman that soon she would feel differently about the other and that the joint sessions would be easier than could be imagined now.

Interestingly, each woman admitted that she wanted the situation to change but didn't think it was even a remote possibility. When I asked each to rate on a scale of 1 to 10 how likely it was they would find a way to work together amicably, their individual answers were 0 and 1. When asked to use the same scale to gauge how important they thought it was for them to resolve this conflict in order to work together and accomplish what they needed to do each day, each said 10. When I asked if each woman was willing to engage in the process and got a "yes" from both, I saw they were committed to giving it their best.

Based on our initial conversation and interviews with their manager, I could tell Lauren and Susan had the capacity to stay the course. We were off to a good start.

Assess Willingness to Commit

One of the things I realized in early one-on-one coaching experiences is that if the parties are not motivated to change, they won't. I would talk benefits, teach skills, and offer experiences for practical applications, but nothing would sink in. Sometimes people's disdain at having to go through the coaching was evident. Other times, the individuals were better actors and pretended to be involved. I became more intuitive about knowing when my efforts were wasted. Eventually, I built a clause into my coaching agreements stating that if, during the course of the work, I concluded for any reason that coaching was not the best use of our time, I would report this to the person who hired me and we would decide how to proceed. I had come to realize that a willing attitude determined 90 percent of the outcome.

Have you ever tried to resolve a conflict that one of the parties did not want to resolve? Recall one where you didn't want to reach resolution. Perhaps you acted as if you wanted to resolve it and said all the right things, such as, "Let's talk and find a way to move forward" and "I know we can work this out." Perhaps you asked questions and did your best to adopt an inquiring stance, saying things like, "Please tell me how you see it." But nothing seemed to change, because you weren't really interested in resolution if it meant you had to change—and consequently, you didn't commit fully to the process.

In conflict situations, it takes an internal shift to no longer see the other person as the source of the problem. And it takes a strong sense of purpose to consider alternatives to blame and justification. It's difficult to resolve issues when you don't want to do these things. Most of us would rather prove a point, hear an apology, or have our opinion acknowledged in some way.

Your employees may well be struggling with the same resistance to seeing themselves as part of the problem, and they have the same need for validation and support. What would encourage them to resolve their conflict? Why would they want to? What's in it for them?

WIIFM

Are you familiar with the world's most popular radio station: WIIFM—What's In It For Me? When you're tuned to this internal channel, you're fixated on questions such as:

- "Why should I work this out?"

- "How will my job or my life be better, easier, and more enjoyable?"

- "Why should I go through the hassle, heartache, and headache of talking about a situation I'd rather not deal with and struggling to get along with a person I'd rather avoid?"

- ❧ "What will happen if I do listen to the other person?"

- ❧ "What will happen if I don't?"

- ❧ "Do I trust my manager to help?"

- ❧ "Do I trust myself to be able to do what may be asked of me?"

- ❧ "Am I willing to commit to the process?"

- ❧ "Do I trust the other's sincerity and commitment?"

- ❧ "What if the situation gets worse?"

- ❧ "What if we are able to resolve our issues? What would that look like? What if we're not?"

Your employee wants to be able to answer these questions, too. When you can help your people address these kinds of issues, the conflict is headed toward resolution.

Shift from Resistance to Connection

If you really want to rediscover wonder, you need to step outside of that tiny, terrified space of rightness and look around at each other and look out at the vastness and complexity and mystery of the universe and be able to say, "Wow, I don't know. Maybe I'm wrong.
—Kathryn Schulz, "On Being Wrong," TED Talk

We often hear it said that we cannot control others, and for the most part, that is true. We cannot force others to be the way we want them to be. But, because we are in relationship with them, because we're connected, they will be affected by our choice to breathe and become more centered.
—Judy Ringer, *Unlikely Teachers*

Humans can be stubborn. We resist change because we think it means something about us is wrong, and we don't like to be wrong. As much as we want to resolve conflict and create a life and workplace that is comfortable and productive, there are obstacles and hidden objectives:

- ❧ When the choice seems to be about being right or wrong, I prefer being right.

    ⇛ If working on the conflict means looking at my contribution to it, I'd rather take a pass.

    ⇛ Although resolution might make life easier, there are benefits to the status quo that I've identified with. For example, I feel superior in my "rightness" or I like playing the victim card.

In the aikido metaphor and in actual practice, the aikidoist learns quickly that the feeling of resistance from my partner equates with ineffective technique—I'm doing something wrong. When aikido is done well, it flows. My partner gives energy, and I receive it; then I give and he receives. Power transfers back and forth in an effortless flow.

This back-and-forth with a partner feels great and is what aikido is all about. But it doesn't always happen. Sometimes I partner with someone who is tense or resistant, making the technique more difficult than it needs to be. It's normal to tighten up in the presence of an attack. What's interesting is that the more my partner stiffens, the tighter I become, especially as I attempt to "correct" him. "He's not falling right! If he'd only loosen up a little, he could feel what I want him to do! Oh, he'll never get it. He's just too tight!"

When I notice that I'm becoming tense in response to my partner, I'm forced to ask if my partner's tension is actually in response to me. What if he thinks I'm resistant? In life off the mat, for example, have you ever complained about someone to a friend, saying, "I can't believe how defensive he is. All I get is pushback!" You learn quickly in aikido that resistance doesn't cause itself. Perhaps the person you're complaining about is saying the same about you!

The good news is, if I relax, my partner will, too. Because of the depth of the connection between us, it only takes one of us to make a change that both of us experience.

In the workplace, the physical tension of conflict is less obvious but it's there nonetheless. If I need to be right, my conflict partner will most likely also want to be right. The more I try to prove my point, the harder they push back. This kind of resistance manifests in the workplace as heated arguments, emotional outbursts, and verbal attacks, as well as unreturned emails, unfinished projects, negativity, duplicity, justification ("They're the problem; I'm doing everything I can!"), avoidance ("No, really, everything is fine"), and other forms of passive aggression.

Brain Science

We receive so much internal and external reinforcement for being on the right side of an issue that we do almost anything to stay there. In her book *Conversational Intelligence,* Judith Glaser shares compelling research showing that when we win an argument, our brain releases feel-good chemicals, such as adrenaline and dopamine. We can become addicted to this feeling and actually seek out conflict because when we win, we feel content, glad, and cheerful.

Fortunately, the brain also releases oxytocin, another feel-good chemical that is associated with human connection. We can leverage this feeling state by listening to, acknowledging, and having empathy for others. Likewise, the more we are listened to and have our words acknowledged, the more we feel liked and trusted and want to offer these feelings in return.

So, how do you help your people see the addiction to being right for what it is, and encourage them to move toward relationship, empathy, and acknowledgment—even in situations when that person is right? How do you support your employees in moving from resistance to connection?

One way is to help people in conflict understand how the current situation developed and how, by resolving it, they can have a future that's more satisfying, powerful, and advantageous to their careers. The individual sessions are designed to do exactly this. First, however, we need to find out if the parties are willing to commit and have the ability to change.

Resistant Versus Connecting Language

The key ingredient to a successful outcome in our coaching process is the willingness of the parties to fully engage. Unwillingness is a non-starter.

This commitment can be difficult to assess for a number of reasons: The parties may appear willing in order to please management.

They may also hope that, as the process unfolds, management discovers the other party is at fault. Although these aren't the best reasons to enter into the process, each offers a place to start. As you go along, you can determine if the parties are willing to commit beyond appearances and the false hope of not having to change themselves.

In conflict, the predominant story people hold is that everything would be great if the other person were different. It's crucial to begin early on to help the parties understand the error inherent in this thinking and construct a new narrative.

When our well-being is dependent on someone else behaving in a certain way, our focus is outward and our actions are contingent on things we have no control over. In this circumstance, we inadvertently lose power and waste energy.

In aikido, we learn this concept in physical ways. For example, when my partner won't move, I may try to force him by pushing or pulling, which only increases his resistance and the potential for injury. The harder I push, the harder my partner pushes back.

Instead of trying to force my partner to move, I can locate the source of the push, move myself out of the way, and then blend with and redirect the push energy. Now, there's no resistance because I'm no longer there to push against. By moving, I change resistance into connection.

The act of moving myself instead of forcing another is just as counterintuitive on the mat as it is in life. It feels as if I'm giving away an advantage, whereas the opposite is true. It takes practice to understand how much we gain when we learn to move our position in order to see more clearly.

In life, I "move myself" when I invite my conflict partner to tell me more about his or her thinking on a topic that I feel very differently about. Resistance sounds like, "Yeah, but . . . " or "No, you don't understand." Connection sounds like, "Can you say more about your thinking on this?" Ask yourself: What kind of language is more likely to solve the problem?

Examples of Resistant Versus Connecting Language

Pushback/Resistance	Entering/Blending/Connection
"Yeah, but . . .	"Can you say more?"
"No, you don't understand!"	"Please help me understand."
"That won't work."	"I'm not sure I agree. I'd like to hear your reasons."
"That's ridiculous!"	"I'm curious; why do you think so?"

As their coach, I invite the parties to understand this concept of "push equals pushback" every time they start to blame someone else. I bring them back to the fact that the only power they have is within themselves—their mindset, their actions, and their ability to change. I suggest they see fault, blame, and justification as indications that they're weakening their position. In essence, we maintain control of our choices and actions by giving up the false notion of control we think we have over the other.

In Chapter 5, the *Aikido Off the Mat: Tenkan* exercise helps the parties physically experience and integrate this concept. As the parties step away from the need to control through blame and justification, they free up energy and understand the conflict from a broader perspective.

Aikido Off the Mat: Conflict as a Gift

A key belief and teaching in conflict resolution is that conflict can be useful—an opportunity to learn, grow, and gain a new perspective on something. As author and aikidoist Thomas Crum writes,

*"Conflict just is. It's what we do with it that makes the difference."
If we decide it will be terrible, it will. If we choose a mindset of
learning and fascination, we encounter less stress and more fascination. If we think of the other person as an adversary, we contribute in subtle and not so subtle ways to sustaining an adversarial
relationship. If we think, "Wow, thank you very much!" and start
looking for the gift, we eventually find it.*

*Kurt Vonnegut uses the phrase "wrang-wrangs" to describe
great teachers who are placed in our life disguised as difficult people. "Wrang-wrangs" are placed there on purpose, he says, to teach
us important lessons.*

*In aikido, when we refer to the attack as a "gift of energy," we
change the locus of power from the attacker ("Oh no! He's coming
for me!") to the receiver ("Ah, yes. Energy I can use!"). When we
imagine the possibility of this energy as a gift, we change from
being fearful to being curious, which is the mindset connected to
growth and learning. Helping your employees adopt the concept
that conflict is neutral—and that it's up to each of us to find the
gift in conflict—helps the conflict resolution process immeasurably
and provides a foundational metaphor for your work.*

What to Watch For

I'm usually able to determine each person's motivation and willingness to change in my first session with them. For example, I watch
non-verbal communication. Is the person:

- Smiling or frowning?
- Nodding or looking away?
- Listening or ignoring me?
- Engaged or bored?
- Sustaining eye contact or appearing distracted?

I also notice if the person:

- Asks questions that show interest and understanding.
- Shows any emotions or reaction as I talk about what they
  can look forward to in the process.

I ask specific questions to get a sense of the parties' optimism and willingness, and to generate conversation:

- ல் "On a scale of 1 to 10, how important is it to your work/team/organization that you and your coworker resolve this conflict?"

- ல் "On a scale of 1 to 10, how optimistic are you about resolving the conflict? What is the reason behind that number?"

- ல் "On a scale of 1 to 10, what is your willingness to resolve these issues? What is your commitment to this process?"

- ல் "What are you most eager to learn as we go forward?"

- ல் "What are you most concerned/anxious/hopeful about?"

- ல் "What would help you personally?"

I ask the second and third questions again just before moving into the joint sessions, after the parties have developed some skills and new perspective. It's fascinating to watch the scales move.

Recall that you may hear answers such as, "I'm very willing, but she'll never change" or "I'm doing everything I can already. She's the problem." These statements tell you the person doesn't understand his contribution or his power to affect the outcome. In these cases, you have an opportunity to intervene. For example, you might respond:

> I know it seems that way, and yet while that kind of thinking—"If only they would change, everything would be great"—may be true, it doesn't solve the problem. In fact, it weakens you. As long as your happiness is dependent on external events being perfect, you waste energy trying to change things you have no ability to change. We're going to start by focusing on you—on building skills that serve you as a leader and change agent in the organization. These capabilities will eventually help you solve any conflict that arises. Sound good?

Aikido Off the Mat: A Transfer of Skills

Here is an example of aikido's primary principle: blend and redirect. It is also an example of encouraging someone with abundant capacity in one area of her work to increase her commitment and capacity to change in other areas, leading to tangible benefits.

Working some years ago with two midlevel leaders, it became clear that one, Alison, had the capacity to change but not the commitment. Although she was a star in the customer service arena, Alison had poor relationships with the majority of her colleagues. She had some awareness of her part in the difficulty but was unmotivated to modify her behavior. Alison was such an important performer for the organization, there was little chance she would face consequences significant enough to faze her. She solved service problems successfully and had excellent customer relationships.

I could see Alison was a born high achiever who wanted to excel at everything, and I began the coaching process by appreciating what was already working. She was a customer service rock star. How did she do it? How did she build such strong relationships with her customers and yet show no interest in doing the same thing with colleagues?

We looked at how she developed rapport, respect, and trust; how these skills served her in gaining referrals and repeat business; and why it might be worth looking at employing these same competencies in the office. A quick study, Alison could see her talent as transferable, and in the end, she became more collegial at work because she saw the advantages of more effective interactions with her teammates. And after the fact, she admitted her life at work was less stressful and more enjoyable.

Gain Commitment: The 5 Ps

As one of the last steps in the individual sessions, I foster commitment to the process by looking for ways in which the ongoing conflict gets in people's way. Where are their pain points, and how are they contributing to them? And I invite each party to ask, "What's in it for me?" as a way to move from the current path to a new one. I find the best encouragement for moving to a new path to be a combination of the following motivators—the 5 Ps:

1. Pain

- ✍ Help each party clarify the consequences of continuing the status quo. What are all the possible negative futures that could evolve from the current state of affairs? Help them see the natural result of continuing the conflict.

- ✍ Be clear and consistent about the choices each party has available to them.

2. Pleasure

- ✍ Ask each party to imagine the best possible outcome.

- ✍ Encourage everyone to imagine what it would be like to come to work each day with the problem solved. What would be different? Less stress? More cooperation, freedom, productivity?

3. Purpose

- ✍ Paint a picture of where the organization is going—its strengths, future, and mission in the world. How do these individuals complete this picture? What are their roles in carrying the vision forward? What's needed from them?

- ✍ Connect with their purpose for joining the company.

- ✍ Connect with their life purpose. What do you know of their goals, visions, hopes, and dreams? Are they high achievers? What matters to each of them? Ask questions to learn more about what kind of work the parties enjoy most and what inspires them.

4. Performance and Productivity

- ✍ Help all parties see the coaching process as an investment in their futures with the organization. Being asked to undergo this process is a vote of confidence in an individual's future contribution, not a punishment.

5. Personal Power

    ᴄᴠ   Explain how the process can improve each party's ability to manage conflict in all areas of life by acquiring the skills to make work more enjoyable as well as to see conflict as a gift and a teacher.

> *My friend and colleague Fran Liautaud, the head of training and development at Maine Drilling and Blasting, relayed the following story to me.*
>
> *"As a manager, if you are going to ask people to resolve their conflict, you have to be a non-judgmental, non-directive leader, because you are leading the process.*
>
> *"I learned this early in my career, when I was the director of production services at a large events-management firm. I had two senior producers who had worked together for about ten years. When I came on board, they had a lot of conflict. They'd lost the ability to work well together, and the company paid a price because their projects often fell short of excellence.*
>
> *"They were both valued employees and both fantastic at their craft. But they couldn't get along, and I realized we had to address this.*
>
> *"They were both leery. Each had decided there was no way they could get along. Plus, they didn't care about what the other person had to say, and they didn't think they would be able to see a different perspective. But because the alternative was to continue in disharmony, which was also proving to be hard on them, each decided she would be willing to get involved in the process."*

Develop Ability

If you want something new, you have to stop doing something old.
—Peter F. Drucker

Willingness and ability are different, and it's possible to have one without the other. As we've seen, being willing to commit is an inside job. It can be encouraged in someone else but not mandated. Ability, however, can be developed in others if they have the commitment to make it happen. Ability to address conflict manifests as competence and skillfulness in self-reflection, interpersonal communication, and empathy, as well as other similar learned habits of mind, body, and spirit.

We develop new conflict habits in a similar way to how we change any other habit. If I want to stop smoking, I need to replace the habit of smoking with a new one—not smoking. I begin by increasing my awareness of the urge to smoke and my physical habit of reaching for a cigarette. I notice the entrenched internal dialogue that supports the habit ("Just this one . . .") and begin to replace it with a new one ("If you refrain this time, it will be easier next time, and gradually you'll be a healthier person.") Over time, I replace the smoking habit with a non-smoking habit.

We don't always see conflict habits in the same way. Nor do we often see the choices available in conflict. These choices are not as obvious as reaching for a cigarette or eating an extra ice cream bar. But the way the patterns grow and affect us are the same.

In his revelatory book *The Power of Habit*, Charles Duhigg explains exactly how habits are formed and, consequently, how we can undo them by forming new ones. In his entertaining "How to Break Habits" video about the book, Duhigg explains:

> Every habit functions the same way. At first there's a cue, some type of trigger that makes the behavior unfold automatically. Studies tell us that a cue can be a location, a time of day, a certain emotional state, other people, or just a pattern of behaviors that consistently triggers a certain routine.

Because we're habituated to certain ways of behaving, when triggered by the conflict cue, we react as we've been patterned to. If I want to engage differently in conflict, I begin by noticing the pattern that leads to the actions I want to change. Our coaching method involves unraveling this process and helping the parties see the cues that trigger their unconscious patterns, so they can pause and consider new actions to move in a more purposeful direction.

The following are examples of typical conflict habits and ways we might re-pattern them into more effective choices.

Old Habit	New Pattern
In conflict, I accommodate until my back is against the wall, and then I explode.	I know I'm a people pleaser and often over accommodate. I have learned to watch for this pattern and ask myself if what I'm agreeing to is actually okay with me.
When I'm irritated, I shut down.	When I become irritated, I notice physical tension, which is a signal that I'm about to shut down. I break the pattern with a conscious breath. This helps me stay open and talk things out.
I avoid conflict at all costs.	When I start taking things too personally, I remember to get curious, ask a question, and try to see the other person's view.
I try to make sure no one is hurt by conflict. I like everyone to be happy.	When others become emotional, I center myself and listen.

Have you noticed any of these habits in your team? What new habits would be useful for each of the parties in your scenario? What would it take for them to change? These are useful questions and thought exercises in the individual sessions.

Willingness and ability are related. If the parties are willing, then it's likely they will be able to learn and build skills. Occasionally, you may learn that an individual has limited ability even though they have strong motivation. If the person is unable to pick up on their teammates' verbal or non-verbal social cues, such as facial expressions and body language, they will find it more difficult to sense meaning and intention in others and to alter their behavior in response. Where possible, obtaining permission to talk with other managers or peers with whom an employee works or interacts helps you get a sense of their ability. You're investing in this process because you believe the parties are worth your time and energy. If they are willing to commit to the process, you will help them develop their skill and ability during the individual sessions.

Aikido Off the Mat: What If . . .

The first individual session with each party may be the most important. You are seeking to accomplish a great deal: You're listening to their stories of the conflict, fully and non-judgmentally, and giving them the opportunity to air it and let it go. You are also assessing the individual's willingness and ability to engage in a process of resolving the conflict through skill development, empathy, and problem-solving.

If you're asking yourself whether to invest the time and energy required by the four-phase process, the answers to the following questions can help you decide:

- ∽ *What is the worth of the parties' expertise and value to the company? What would it cost to replace one or both?*

- ∽ *In your view, after meeting with each party individually, is the relationship repairable or beyond repair?*

- ∽ *In your view, are the parties willing to change? Will they develop the skills and ability necessary to do so?*

- ∽ *Is one or more of the parties so resistant or identified with their position that they continually revert to blame, justification, and other intransigent behaviors?*

- ∽ *Would either of the parties be described as "toxic" to the organization as a whole?*

If one or both of the parties refuse to see their contribution, or are affecting the organization or team in ways that limit cohesiveness and productivity, keeping these individuals on staff may do more harm than good. Even though they are valuable in other ways, their presence affects the environment and holds back what might otherwise be a high-functioning team. Not everyone can work together harmoniously. If you find this is the case, it may be best to separate the individuals involved and move on.

Additionally, if you believe you may be contributing to the conflict in some way, or have other doubts about managing the intervention, I suggest talking with an HR professional about who may be more suitable. In my experience, it is difficult to play the role of coach when unraveling a conflict that involves you.

If you decide to proceed with the process, the first individual session is a highly reliable indicator of the likelihood of success. What you learn here gives you a sense of how many sessions might be necessary, based on the parties' willingness and abilities. You may decide the parties are willing to move forward and possess enough skills that they only need one individual session each. In this case, I offer a "lite" version of the four-phase approach in Appendix C.

It's also possible you find that you would rather bring in an outside coach because of the parties' high value to the organization, the entrenched nature of the conflict, and/or the skill required to facilitate the process.

The benefit to working with the parties yourself is that you have a chance to practice the skills, attitudes, and behaviors you're introducing. You increase your personal leadership presence and ability to manage the stress of everyday conflict. As such, this important aspect of your job becomes easier and more satisfying.

Identify Conversation Catalysts

In deciding how to go forward, it helps to ask questions in this first session that encourage the parties to tell their stories and allow you to gain some sense of how willing they might be to hear another story later. Of all the intervention techniques I use, asking open, honest questions from a place of curiosity is the most useful. By "honest," I mean questions I don't know the answer to. This is not easy. Just by choosing a question, we make a statement. Why that question and not another? I'm always watching myself for "advocacy disguised as inquiry," as Harvard professor Amy Edmondson calls it. Questions that begin with "Don't you think it would be better if . . .?" or "Do you want to . . .?" or "What if we tried . . .?" sound like questions, but are really statements. We all do it.

In addition to the questions already outlined in previous chapters, the following are examples of questions that are (as much as possible) honest, keeping you in a non-judgmental, curious, and supportive place.

Questions that Broaden the Topic or Learning

- ღ "Can you tell me what's going on?"
- ღ "What is your perspective on how this got started?"
- ღ "What do you need from (the other party)?"
- ღ "How do you feel about doing this work?"
- ღ "What concerns do you have about the process?"
- ღ "What questions do you have for me?"
- ღ "Any other reactions or thoughts?"

Questions that Deepen the Topic or Learning

- ღ "Can you name some reasons you think the problem is resolvable/unresolvable?"
- ღ "What is the concern behind your view?"
- ღ "Can you explain that further?"
- ღ "What happens when you get irritated?"
- ღ "Can you give examples of that?"
- ღ "Have you ever had coaching or training like this before?"
- ღ "What would be helpful for you personally?"
- ღ "What would help you be your best self when conflict arises?"

Any of these questions gets the conversation started. If you listen well, more questions flow from the employee's answers until you find the source of the problem and begin to see what kind of support is needed.

Document the Session

In each session, I take careful notes that I summarize in bullet form. At the end of the session, I email my summary to each of the parties separately. This helps me prepare for the next session. It also lets the people in the conflict review what they said and note recurring patterns as the sessions move forward. The bullets are short and often word for word. I sometimes quote the person. Most participants comment on how helpful they find the written notes.

These notes also help if you decide with the parties (or because their manager has requested it) to create a letter of agreement in which the parties state specific assurances to each other, ways to manage potential setbacks, requests for management support, and possible consequences for not keeping the agreement. A final agreement is usually not a prerequisite to the intervention, but I like to know at the outset. We'll come back to this is Chapter 8.

Before I leave this session, I set a time for the next one and express gratitude for the person's willingness to engage in the process. I also explain that I will send a follow-up email with a summary of my notes and suggested homework to be completed before we meet again. A day or two before the next session, I send a reminder email with the time of the session and the homework assignment.

Homework Examples

- *Managing Conflict with Power & Presence Workbook:* Review through page 5.
- Read "Create a Learning Conversation" in *Difficult Conversations.*
- Read "Thank You Very Much" in *Unlikely Teachers.*
- Come to the next session with three things you appreciate about your conflict partner.

Examples of follow-up emails that include my notes and suggestions for homework are included in Appendix D.

Key Points

- The purpose of the first individual session is to find out if the parties have the ability to change and are willing to commit to the process.
- In conflict situations, it takes an internal shift to not see the other person as the source of the problem.

- The key ingredient to a successful outcome is the willingness of the parties to fully engage.

- When our well-being is dependent on others behaving in a certain way, we lose power and waste energy.

- A key belief and teaching in conflict resolution is that conflict can be an opportunity to learn, grow, and see what the conflict is trying to show us.

- The 5 Ps—pain, pleasure, purpose, performance, and personal power—can be useful for gaining the parties' commitment.

- Developing skillfulness in conflict situations is about developing new conflict habits.

- The first individual session may be the most important and is a reliable indicator of the likelihood of success of the conflict resolution process.

- By practicing the skills and behaviors you're introducing, you increase your personal leadership presence and ability to manage everyday conflict.

- The parties benefit by receiving a summary of your notes in a follow-up email.

Sources

- *Working with Difficult People: Turn Tormentors Into Teachers* by Judy Ringer, *www.judyringer.com*

- "How to Break Habits," *https://www.youtube.com*

Aikido flow videos

- Judy Ringer, "Conflict As an Opportunity," *https://www.youtube.com/watch?v=cZ6RNLhFARg*

- Judy Ringer, "Judy Ringer Aikido Flow," *https://www.youtube.com/watch?v=NdOSmHE_GCY*

The centered state is a conscious choice.

4 DEVELOP POWER AND PRESENCE

When you change, everything changes.
—Judy Ringer

Primary Purpose

Chapter 4's purpose is to give the parties ways to effectively change their mind-body state to one of optimal performance and emotional awareness. You help both parties experience the difference between a centered and an uncentered state as well as how to choose the centered state anytime, anywhere.

Preparation

- ☙ Know the purpose and desired outcome for the session.
- ☙ Know which skills you will focus on and why.
- ☙ Have scenarios in mind for role-playing and practicing the skills.
- ☙ Read your notes from the previous session.
- ☙ Enter with optimism for a positive outcome.

Agenda

- ☙ Express gratitude for the person's presence.
- ☙ Explain your hopes for the session and ask them about theirs.

- ✑ Ask for any developments since the last session.
- ✑ Teach centered presence and purposeful power.
- ✑ Use examples from their conflict to practice the skills.
- ✑ Discuss ways to prepare for the next session and set a date.
- ✑ Take notes and send them in a follow-up email after the session.
- ✑ Assign homework.

In a session with Susan, she talked about how frustrating it was when Lauren came back after a few days of vacation. Susan portrayed Lauren as loud and distracting: "She likes to sing to herself and makes noise as she moves around the workspace." Susan didn't yet know how to communicate to Lauren that her behavior was distracting without being angry and rude.

We talked about the roller coaster of emotions and how acknowledging emotional energy helps to defuse it. Emotions happen. Learning how to center yourself doesn't mean your emotions suddenly disappear or you suppress them in some way. We talked about how centering allows you to fully own your emotions and reframe them as energy that can be used in a more purposeful way.

The session was an opening for Susan. She began to see how she could more skillfully communicate her frustration to Lauren about distractions while also appreciating Lauren's enthusiasm and joyful demeanor in the workplace.

Teach Centered Presence

Centering is not an abstract term, but rather a practical tool available to all of us.
—Thomas Crum, *Journey to Center*

In Chapter 1, the focus was on your quality of being—your ability to manage your behavior, mindset, and purpose as you enter the room using the principles of centered presence, personal power, and clarity of purpose. Here in Chapter 4, you help your employees develop these principles in order to stay calm, centered, open, and respectful when they communicate with their conflict partner. As you teach and coach the parties in these self-management techniques, you are also modeling them and adding new centering practices to your own repertoire.

When teaching conflict and communication skills, I envision two concentric circles. The outside circle is the container for our **quality of being skills:** centered presence, personal power, and clarity of purpose. The inner circle—surrounded and supported by our quality of being—holds our **communication skills:** inquiry, active listening, acknowledgement, advocacy, and problem-solving.

Quality of Being Skills

In large part, the intervention you are undertaking is about deepening people's awareness of the influence they have moment to moment and their capacity to respond purposefully and skillfully under pressure. You are refining personal and professional intentions—yours and those of the parties you're coaching.

We are talking about **quality of being:** the underlying tone of my actions—including the way I carry myself physically, mentally, and emotionally—as well as the awareness with which I approach a conflict. Am I centered and breathing? Do I understand my part in influencing the conversation? How do I manage my emotional energy? Can I step back, witness myself in action, and make conscious choices? Our physical posture, breath, and composure influence our thinking and the environment around us.

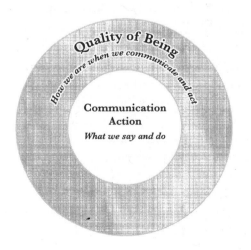

Quality of Being
How we are when we communicate and act

Communication
Action
What we say and do

Communication Skills

Communication skills refer to what I say and do—that is, the ways in which I express my views, listen actively to others, and collaborate on solutions (or not). A skilled communicator knows how to keep the dialogue psychologically safe, focused on the task at hand, and moving in a positive direction. (These skills are covered in Chapter 5.)

We begin with quality of being because being "speaks" louder than doing. The underlying principles of presence, power, and purpose are most evident here and are necessary for the communication strategies to be effective. Thomas Crum puts it this way: "Quality of being is primary. Everything else is secondary." Crum is describing a state of mind-body-spirit—the most crucial and most neglected element in difficult communication. The best content and delivery skills always are betrayed by an uncentered state, which is why we begin here and will continually return to this skill set.

Centering and the Learning Mindset

As we learned in Chapter 1, a core component of centered presence is the mindset with which you approach a conflict or difficult conversation, and is a concept I reinforce throughout the process.

As a general practice, I want the parties to re-center periodically in order to stay in a learning frame of mind. In more specific applications, such as a difficult conversation, participants learn that when they're centered, they're also present, flexible, curious, and aware—all valuable qualities under pressure. Aikido says we can handle the energy of the attack only by being open to moving off our current position to one in which we can see where the energy is coming from and where it's going. From this vantage point, we can join the energy and influence it. A fixed position—or an inflexible mindset—offers no room for enlightenment and, in the martial sense, is a dangerous space to occupy. We don't see what's coming and can't get out of the way.

In her book *Mindset, The New Psychology of Success,* Stanford University psychologist Carol Dweck presents convincing research on two ways of being in the world—the growth mindset and the fixed mindset—and how it's our mindset that really helps us to achieve success and live happier lives.

According to Dweck, mindset trumps ability, talent, and skill in influencing our willingness and ability to change. Her research suggests we are born with a love of learning, which she calls a growth mindset. With encouragement, this capacity continues through life, and is evident in people who love challenge, think of obstacles as opportunities to course correct, and are willing to do what it takes to achieve their purpose. Failure is merely an opening to acquire new skills or perspectives.

Through a combination of nature and nurture, a different mindset can develop that is more rigidly focused on position and the need to win and own the "truth." This is the fixed mindset in which people don't experiment or explore unfamiliar ideas because they fear failure and judgment.

The growth mindset says knowledge and ability can be developed, and consequently, a person with this mindset is naturally more curious and open to hearing other points of view. Someone with a fixed mindset believes that people's abilities are preset and unchanging, and therefore sees a mistake as cause for judgment—of self or others. It's difficult for a person with this mindset to be open to hearing new and different ideas, especially when these conflict with predetermined beliefs.

You can see why it's crucial to reinforce a growth mindset in the people you're managing and coaching. Their mindset frames whether they perceive the external world as judge or teacher, as well as the narratives running inside their heads. In a fixed mindset, the internal monologue is constantly assessing: "I don't want to look bad" and "How can I show I'm right in doing what I did?" A person with a growth mindset, while also monitoring externals, is more likely to ask: "What am I learning here about how this conflict developed?" and "How can I improve my awareness so this doesn't happen again?"

Sharing and encouraging the concept and characteristics of the growth mindset with your employees helps them resolve conflict as well as work together productively in this process and everywhere in their lives.

Characteristics of the Fixed and Growth Mindsets

Fixed Mindset	Growth Mindset
Emotionally reactive	Emotionally responsive and open
More interested in winning an argument than learning from it	More interested in learning than in being right
Seeking constant approval	Open to feedback
Judgmental of self and others	Appreciative of self and others
Usually pessimistic about outcome	Optimistic about the outcome
Blame oriented, unable to see their contribution to the conflict	Curious and open to seeing their contribution
Insistent on getting their way	Looking to achieve a balanced solution

Conflict can intensify the fixed mindset, because I think I look better if I can prove my point.

There are ways to encourage a growth mindset. As the coach, you can help an employee by inviting him to think of a past conflict he solved and learned from. Working with conflict in this way can significantly aid development of a growth mindset and improve quality of life. For example, the growth mindset allows people to view conflict as follows: I have an obstacle. What can I learn from my part in it? What have I learned from past experiences like this? Where's the gift that sets me free from similar conflicts and teaches me how to be a more skilled, professional, and collaborative colleague, partner, or family member?

Another way I encourage a growth mindset is by asking all parties to assume the other person might know something they don't. I often ask them to imagine that the conflict partner grew up on another planet. Then I ask if they would be curious about that planet. The smile or laughter that generally follows such a suggestion automatically shifts us into a growth mindset.

Dweck suggests encouraging the growth mindset by praising employees who take on difficult tasks and see them through, who struggle and succeed in learning something new, who persevere through a setback, or who are open to criticism.

You can assign homework that helps the employee create more learning experiences. For example, invite each party to notice any defensiveness between sessions. Ask if it's helping or holding them back. Once aware of it, each person can channel any defensive energy in a more useful direction, such as talking about the defensiveness with the other person.

We also change by being exposed to constructive role models as well as through new ways of thinking about failure and challenge. Watching you—the coach—maintain curiosity and positivity in the face of difficulty encourages the same in your employees. By doing this, you're teaching skills that are valuable in all areas of life, and you're preparing the parties for joint problem-solving.

The Art of Centering

After talking about centered presence and personal power with Lauren, I showed her an activity that helped her understand physically the difference between being centered and uncentered. With both of us side by side in a standing position, and with Lauren's permission, I pushed on her sternum gently with the flat of my hand, the pressure of my hand representing a conflict, difficult person, or other stressor. The light pressure made Lauren wobble. "The way you feel now," I said, "is the uncentered state and mimics the internal 'wobble' we feel when we react to conflict."

Then I helped her find the centered state by asking her to breathe in and out from her body's center of mass—an internal point just below the navel. I also asked her to redirect the energy of my push toward her center. When I pushed again, she was stable— same pressure, no wobble. Lauren noticed a dramatic difference. She felt physically stable, but also emotionally balanced after she centered herself. Centering is more than an intellectual awareness. When we're centered, mind, body, and spirit are aligned. We feel balanced, stable, and in control.

We talked about centering practices Lauren could add to her daily routine. Examples included making time at the beginning of the day for deep breathing and meditation, as well as remembering to center herself before entering the office and on the way home. She practiced between sessions, and when we next met, she told me she'd become much more aware of her uncentered state, which she described as:

- *Anxious*

- *Shoulders up*

- *Internal dialogue on high*

- *Worry*

I asked what she does now when she notices her shoulders up or her internal dialogue on high. Lauren said, "I take a breath and re-center, so that whatever I do next will be an intentional choice."

Learning to practice centering and learning that the centered state is a conscious choice was foundational to Lauren's ability to connect her actions to the outcome of an interaction. She began to see how she contributed to past conflict and how she could contribute differently in the future.

Centering is the most important of all aspects of our process. Often described as a mind-body state that enhances awareness, centering increases your connection with your environment, promotes flexible thinking, and encourages a growth mindset. Athletes speak of it as "the zone" or "peak performance." Fighter pilots call it "situational awareness," the ability to make the best choice under extreme pressure. When you're centered, you're stable and flexible, balanced and directed, powerful and open. You are present to your surroundings and able to move in whatever direction you choose. You have options you would not normally have in conflict settings.

Most importantly, you have the ability to observe yourself in the process of reacting to conflict, and to intentionally stop the reaction and come back to a more aware, composed, and responsive mind-body state. You do this by focusing on a centering thought, such as the feeling of breathing in and out, a positive image, or your center of gravity.

In terms of how you share this concept with your people, if you can center yourself, you can teach it. You do this by tuning in to the way in which you center yourself, and sharing your method as clearly and specifically as possible. I'll also give you some hints.

To begin, all that's required is a conversation about the concept. I usually start by asking, "What does it mean to be centered?" or "How would you complete this sentence: 'When I'm centered, I'm . . .'" Answers usually include:

- Calm
- Balanced
- In control
- Confident
- Present
- Happy
- Flexible
- Grounded
- Ready
- At peace

I ask for situations in which the individual has been centered or uncentered, and what happened in each case. "Do you believe you have the ability to choose the centered state? If yes, how have you done it? How have you come back from uncenteredness?"

I often hear:

- "I take a deep breath."
- "I count to ten."
- "I think of someone I love."
- "I stop my chattering mind."
- "I feel my feet on the ground."
- "I smile to myself and remember life is bigger than this conflict."

When I teach centering, I want to help the individual understand:

1. **The difference between being centered and uncentered.**
   How does my partner know they're centered? Is it physical (calm/relaxed), mental (curious/open), visual (beach/mountain), kinesthetic (rooted/stable), auditory (song/quiet), or a combination? Each person has a unique way of anchoring the centered state.

2. **That centering requires only intention.** The individual doesn't have to leave the room, take a walk, or meditate. Although these are excellent centering practices, we want to be able to stop, breathe, and center at any moment without requiring changing location.

3. **That centering is a choice.** You will help them understand that centering isn't a wish or a hope, but a mind-body choice they can make at any time.

The key is to make sure the individual experiences the difference between being centered and uncentered, because this provides a reference point they can return to at any time. You want them to anchor this choice in body and mind.

At this point in the session, it's helpful to debrief with the person you're working with by discussing the reason for the practice and the benefits of centering. For example, when you're centered, you are able to:

- Notice your reaction and be grateful for the awareness.
- Stop and gather yourself. You can feel your feet on the floor, conscious breathing from your core, and flowing energy.
- Return to your purpose and act with intention.

Note: It's not enough to merely talk about the concept of centering. Most people know they want to be centered/grounded/balanced/in control, but our reactive patterns are strong. We can't access the state under pressure unless we've practiced it enough to choose it at any time. Use the *Aikido Off the Mat: A Centering Practice* exercise on this page to help your employee distinguish between the two states and recognize the centered state as a mind-body choice available at all times.

In his book *Journey to Center,* Thomas Crum describes personal life adventures in which his ability to center himself played a crucial and, on more than one occasion, a life-saving role. In particular, his story entitled "Centered Relationship" examines what it means to deeply connect with another person, whether it be a loved one or a chance meeting; the ways in which centering increases compassion and presence; and how to practice and attain this kind of mindful relationship in a "quick-fix" world. Crum is a great storyteller, and I encourage you to check out the story and the book.

Aikido Off the Mat: A Centering Practice

How do you practice centering? If you have ways you can share with the parties, please do. If you don't or if you want to add to your collection, it's best to start with the basics, such as breathing in and out, slowly and consciously, for several seconds.

Sharing the idea and practice of centering can be that simple because we are usually not breathing when we're in conflict. Just noticing that you're not breathing and starting again is a simple, yet powerful, centering practice.

Here are some practices you can implement for yourself and share with the conflicting parties. The advantage to these practices is that the parties have a physical experience you can test. As reinforcement (and with permission), try pushing gently on the individual you're working with before and after one of the following centering techniques. When people are uncentered, they'll be unstable and wobbly. When people are in the centered state, they are calm, stable, and reflective, and won't feel as much pressure from your push. Your partner may even ask if you're pushing as hard.

ღ ***Focus on your center of gravity.** You can train yourself to center by standing or sitting in a relaxed posture and focusing on your physical center of gravity—an internal point just below the navel. In aikido, we call it "one-point." We imagine our energy organizing around this one-point and extending out into the world. We walk from center, speak from center, and generally operate from center. In physics, it's our center of mass; in Japanese, it's called* tanden.

ღ ***Breathe with awareness.** Breathe into this one-point. Breathe out from the same point. You will feel more composed, confident, and balanced physically and emotionally. Breathe consciously, and feel the air flow in easily through your nose, head, throat, and lungs, and then deep into your abdomen. Hear the sound the breath makes, and feel it as it flows in and out. Sit quietly for a few minutes and relax your mind.*

ღ ***Start your day centered.** Physical exercise, deep breathing, meditation, prayer, and quiet reflection are all excellent centering practices to begin your day. You may have your own. It can be as simple (and challenging!) as sitting quietly and doing nothing. By starting your day with a centering activity, you can return to the centered state more easily as the day unfolds.*

ღ ***Create centering prompts.** These can include objects, behaviors, people, or events that remind you to re-center periodically. Place posters or quotations on the wall or at your desk that reinforce your practice. Keep a book of affirmations close at hand, or a picture of a loved one to help you remember what is important. Listen to one of your favorite*

*centering audiobooks as you drive to and from work. When
you push open the door to your office, let it be a reminder
to center yourself.*

ᘓ *Choose one practice. As we've said, new habits need reinforcement if they are going to be part of our lives. Choose
one centering practice and incorporate it into your day.
Make a promise to do it for thirty days. Keep track and be
specific. For example: "Each time the phone rings, I will
take a breath and exhale before I answer."*

As a way to reinforce centering and give each party a way to practice it in the workplace, I invite the person to talk about a situation in
which they have a reaction to their conflict partner and become uncentered. I have them think through the last time this happened and ask:

ᘓ "How would becoming centered in that situation have
helped?"

ᘓ "When is the next time this situation is likely to happen?"

ᘓ "How will you remember to center yourself?"

ᘓ "How will this help?"

As part of the homework assignment, I ask each person to keep
a conflict journal in which they can record what happened, how they
reacted, if they centered themselves, and what happened as a result.
The stories they bring back are often amazing.

*Susan said she had a breakthrough with Lauren after our session
on centering, power, and purpose. She was noticing how she became uncentered in response to some of Lauren's behaviors.*

*One example happened when Susan asked Lauren to email
a file in a particular format, and Lauren frowned and walked
away. Lauren's response was fleeting, but Susan saw it. In the past,
the frown would have sparked feelings of anger and frustration in
Susan and set off a series of reactions, ending in Susan putting on
her earphones and avoiding Lauren for the rest of the day.*

But this time, Susan noticed herself beginning to react. She composed herself with a centering practice—she focused on her breathing—and realized she was merely stating a preference in her request for the file format. She had a positive intention to help their mutual client and was entitled to ask for what she wanted. Now centered, Susan chose to move forward in a positive way by not reacting to the frown, and she later expressed appreciation to Lauren when the file came through in the requested format.

Afterward, Susan reflected on how much energy she might have wasted on this minor conflict, especially when she didn't know the reason for the frown and was only making an assumption about it. Susan saw this was not a situation worth expending energy on and she could let it go. Susan said she was becoming more and more aware of her personal power to respond intentionally by finding her center before blurting out something she would probably regret later.

Teach Personal Power

Choice of attention—to pay attention to this and ignore that—is to the inner life what choice of action is to the outer. In both cases, a man is responsible for his choice and must accept the consequences.
—W. H. Auden

When your people understand the potential of the centered state, they also intuitively grasp the concept of personal power as the ability to accomplish purpose. Although this concept can be mysterious at first—What is personal power? Do I have personal power? How do I increase it?—once again, you can give your people an experience of true power in the aikido sense of the word by showing them how to direct their life energy—their ki—literally and figuratively on purpose.

Aikido Off the Mat: Unbendable Arm exercise on page 93 is a fun and persuasive way to demonstrate the connection between personal power and clarity of purpose; when we have one, we have both.

The *Unbendable Arm* exercise is also a powerful exploration of either-or thinking. In *Power and Love,* Adam Kahane, who has authored many books and facilitated conflict resolution worldwide, quotes Martin Luther King Jr. on the subject of power and its often falsely identified opposite, love:

> Power properly understood is nothing but the ability to achieve purpose. . . . And one of the great problems of history is that the concepts of love and power have usually been contrasted as opposites—polar opposites—so that love is identified with the resignation of power, and power with the denial of love.

And later in the quotation:

> Power without love is reckless and abusive, and love without power is sentimental and anemic. . . . It is precisely this collision of immoral power with powerless morality that constitutes the major crisis of our time.

This concept underlies most of our difficulties with one-on-one conflict and our difficulty in identifying personal power. We assume we have to choose between power and love, kindness, or compassion, and the countless manifestations of this choice: getting our way or letting others have theirs, being respectful or being direct, being honest or being loyal, and expressing our point of view or listening to others' views. But these are all false choices.

Personal power and love walk hand in hand. When I'm centered and purposeful, I can:

- Be open to new ways and rooted in principle.
- Be both respectful and direct.
- Choose honesty and loyalty.
- Entertain other viewpoints and express my own.

Similarly, consider the concept "Heart at Peace" in *The Anatomy of Peace* by the Arbinger Institute. This is a simple concept: Do I enter the conflict with a *heart at peace*—a willingness to resolve the problem— or do I enter with a *heart at war* that wants to win regardless of the cost? As with the false choice of power or love, often we equate peace with being soft or overly yielding, which prevents us from choosing peace in conflict. Although war may not be our first choice, at least it's associated with power, reward, and winning—outcomes humans often strive for. But, I encourage myself and my partners to ask: "Are these my only choices—hard or soft, win or lose?"

When we enter a conflict conversation with a heart at peace, and with the understanding that we can engage with power and compassion, we can be open and direct as we try to resolve the problem, knowing the problem won't be fully resolved until all parties feel heard and supported.

As the coach, you reinforce these concepts so the parties can begin to move away from positional thinking, see more clearly how they can work together in a "both-and" world, and increase their personal power.

Teach Clarity of Purpose

True power is energy flowing freely toward a purpose.
—Thomas Crum

In the individual sessions, you also help the conflicting parties develop clarity of purpose. For example:

- What is the purpose of the process they're being asked to engage in?
- What would be an ideal outcome for them?
- Why should they care?
- What's in it for them?
- How does this outcome fit into their larger career and life purpose?

In the opening sessions, it's important to set the scene. If the participants are feeling vulnerable about being invited into a coaching situation, I've found it helpful to be as transparent as possible about my role, what is expected, and the positive aspects to gain from participating fully. To build enthusiasm and motivation, I help participants see what's possible and how they will work together differently when they complete the process.

To further clarify the power each party can gain over conflict and prepare them for the communication strategies around purpose, I use the following *Unbendable Arm* exercise. It's a traditional activity in aikido dojos around the world and common in non-aikido circles as well. The beauty of this exercise is its simplicity in demonstrating the effortlessness of personal power when directed toward a purpose they care about.

Aikido Off the Mat: The Unbendable Arm
(Adapted from *The Magic of Conflict* by Thomas Crum)

1. *Participants choose partners and stand side by side.*

2. *Partner A extends her arm in front of her with her fist closed and thumb side up.*

3. *Partner B stands on the outside and grasps Partner A's arm, one hand under the wrist and the other over the bicep (see illustration).*

4. *Partner B tries to bend Partner A's arm, pushing up on the wrist and down on the bicep with equal pressure. Partner A can allow her arm to bend at a right angle to get a feel for the movement, and then straighten the arm out again.*

5. *Now, Partner A attempts to be so strong that Partner B won't be able to bend her arm. At the same time, Partner A should notice the amount of energy and effort it takes to keep her arm from bending.*

6. *Next, Partner A opens her fist, extends her fingers, and visualizes something or someone of great importance across the room, which represents her passion or purpose. Partner A imagines a stream of ki (energy) flowing through her extended arm and fingers (like water through a fire hose) in the direction of her purpose.*

7. *Partner B resumes trying to bend Partner A's arm in a measured and unhurried fashion, gradually adding back the pressure he used in Step 5.*

8. *Partner B tells Partner A when he has added back as much pressure as he was using in Step 5.*

9. *Partner A's arm should remain extended toward purpose but with considerably less effort. The more Partner A relaxes—as long as she maintains focus on her vision—the stronger the arm becomes.*

You may want to try this activity before using it with people you're coaching. When you feel in your own mind and body the difference between the two ways of being, you are better able to put the metaphor to work. You start to notice that (just like in the exercise) when your focus moves from problem to purpose, you are more focused and powerful with less effort. Obstacles—represented by the pressure on your arm—disappear into the flow of energy heading toward purpose. In fact, the obstacles are a clarifying stimulus, an invitation to refine, simplify, or better identify what it is you really want from this work, life, or conversation.

A second way to demonstrate the power of purpose is to ask the parties to name an activity they love—something where time disappears because they are so persistent and absorbed in the activity. When this happens, a person is in the "flow" state—a highly focused mind-body condition first described by the Hungarian psychologist Mihaly Csikszentmihalyi in *Flow: The Psychology of Optimal Experience.* When in flow, we're more creative and intrinsically motivated than when we're performing a task out of necessity or obligation. In the flow state, we're present in the here and now, we lose ourselves to the task, and we're "on purpose."

In whatever manner you choose, it is essential for you to clarify each person's purpose for the intervention. You must also periodically check in with the participants to determine if the purpose has changed or stayed the same throughout the process.

If participants express doubts or questions such as the following, I invite them to provide their own answers:

- "Why are we doing this?"
- "Why should I continue?"
- "What do I really want from this?"
- "What is my hope for the joint sessions?"

Ideally, the parties have a similar overarching purpose of finding ways to work together more harmoniously, with greater self-awareness, emotion management, and support for each other back at work. When the purpose is clear and frequently reinforced, the parties are largely willing to work toward a sustainable solution.

The power of a clearly defined purpose continues to be a key element of our process, and it will surface again as a crucial stage of The 6-Step Checklist (Chapter 5), which puts purpose into action to transform difficult conversations into learning conversations.

Practice

It took me seven years to become a black belt in aikido, three more to rise to second degree, and ten more to achieve third degree. Similarly, it takes time to learn how to manage conflict and communicate effectively. We weren't born with this knowledge, and practicing these skills can change lives.

The following practice opportunities help the parties reinforce the skills they're learning and prepare them for a new way of working together. They can be assigned as homework, used during the session, or both.

1. **Centered presence:** Ask each person for five stories on centering. In their stories, the participants should note:

   · Times they remembered to center themselves under pressure and what happened as a result.

   · Times they forgot to center themselves when it would have been helpful and what happened as a result.

   · How they will remember to center themselves next time a similar conflict arises.

2. **Personal power:** Help the parties experience the power they have to explore a different viewpoint. When in conflict with someone, it's easy to see only the part of that person that's the problem for us. For example, if I think you're controlling and selfish, I see only control and selfishness. In fact, I begin to look for those behaviors in order to justify my view. I downplay or unconsciously ignore behaviors that might show you to be generous and flexible. To change this mindset:

   · Ask each party to explore the power of changing their view from seeing only the problematic part of their coworker to looking for other parts: the concerned parent, loving grandparent, or close friend.

   · Ask each of the parties to list one behavior or quality they admire in the other.

   · As homework, ask each of the parties to look for additional behaviors or qualities they like or respect in the other, and keep a log for the following session. Each person must list at least three things, and look only for what they admire or respect.

3. **Clarity of purpose:** Ask each party for answers to the following questions:

   · What would be my ideal outcome for this coaching process?

- What do I want for myself?
- What do I want for my conflict partner?
- What outcome would be ideal for my organization, team, or business?
- How would I like to engage differently when the process is complete?

When I first asked Susan and Lauren individually what they appreciated about the other, I got blank stares. I was used to it. People in conflict aren't looking for the positives in their conflict partner; they only see frustration, irritation, and wrong-headed thinking—and they aren't hesitant about relating those. But with some centering, smiling, and silence on my part, they each found something they could sincerely say they appreciated.

ç∂ *Susan's skill on the phone with difficult callers*

ç∂ *How Lauren treated her customers*

ç∂ *High marks from both on each other's work ethic*

Once we opened that particular avenue of exploration, the appreciations flowed more easily, and sometimes I didn't even have to ask.

Homework Examples

ç∂ *Managing Conflict with Power & Presence Workbook:* Review through page 11.

ç∂ Read "Have Your Feelings (or They Will Have You)" and "What's Your Purpose" in *Difficult Conversations* by Douglas Stone, Bruce Patton, and Sheila Heen.

ç∂ Read "Relax!," "Getting on the Mat," and "What Is This Thing Called Ki?" in *Unlikely Teachers* by Judy Ringer.

ç∂ Read "Centered Relationship" in *Journey to Center* by Thomas Crum.

ᑫᕼ Come to the next session with at least three things you admire or respect about [the conflict partner].

ᑫᕼ Look for opportunities to practice centering and notice what happens. Bring stories about centering to the next session.

ᑫᕼ Keep a conflict journal and bring it to the next session. Include:

- What happened?
- How did you handle what happened?
- What did you appreciate about your response?
- What will you do differently next time?

ᑫᕼ Notice any defensiveness that arises between sessions. How is it helping you? How is it holding you back? In what ways might you use this life energy more constructively?

Complete the session by setting a time for the next one and thanking the parties for their hard work. Send a follow-up email with your notes and suggested homework. A day or two before the next session, send a reminder email.

Key Points

ᑫᕼ The purpose behind developing power and presence is to give the parties ways to effectively change their mind-body state to one of optimal performance and emotional awareness.

ᑫᕼ **Quality of being** is the way someone carries herself physically, mentally, and emotionally, and the awareness with which she approaches the conflict.

ᑫᕼ **Communication strategies** are the ways in which someone expresses his views, listens actively to others, and collaborates on solutions.

ᑫᕼ Our quality of being is the most crucial and most neglected element in difficult communication.

- Someone with a growth mindset is open to possibility and knows that ability can be nurtured and developed.

- Someone with a fixed mindset believes that abilities are preset and unchanging.

- Centering is the key to managing emotional energy and adopting a growth mindset.

- Clarity of purpose helps the parties determine what they want and influences their participation in the joint sessions.

- Clarifying each person's purpose for the intervention is essential and should be ongoing.

Sources

- *Power and Love: A Theory and Practice of Social Change* by Adam Kahane

- *The Anatomy of Peace: Resolving the Heart of Conflict* by The Arbinger Institute.

- *Mindset: The New Psychology of Success* by Carol Dweck

- *Journey to Center* by Thomas Crum

- *The Magic of Conflict* by Thomas Crum

- *Flow: The Psychology of Optimal Experience* by Mihaly Csikszentmihalyi

Have you ever worked or dined in a restaurant that has a swinging door in and out of the kitchen? Have you ever pushed (or watched someone push) on that door when another body is trying to get through from the other direction? What happens?

You push, they push, and nobody gets through.

5 Demonstrate Communication Strategies

There's only one way to understand the other person's story, and that's by being curious. Instead of asking yourself, 'How can they think that?!' ask yourself, 'I wonder what information they have that I don't?' Instead of asking, 'How can they be so irrational?' ask, 'How might they see the world such that their view makes sense?' Certainty locks us out of their story; curiosity lets us in.
—Douglas Stone, Bruce Patton, and Sheila Heen, *Difficult Conversations*

Primary Purpose

As the individual sessions continue, your purpose in Chapter 5 is to combine centered presence with key communication strategies in order to change the parties' adversarial dynamic and help them communicate more effectively.

Preparation

- ◌ Know the purpose and desired outcome for the session.
- ◌ Know which skills you will focus on and why.
- ◌ Have scenarios in mind for role-playing and practicing the skills.
- ◌ Read your notes from the previous session.
- ◌ Enter with optimism for a positive outcome.

Agenda

- ◌ Express appreciation for the individual's presence.
- ◌ Explain your hopes for the session and ask what the individual hopes to gain.

    ⇛   Ask for any new developments since the last session.

    ⇛   Teach communication strategies and skills, employing examples from the conflict at hand.

    ⇛   Discuss ways to prepare for the next session and set a date.

    ⇛   Take notes and send them in a follow-up email after the session.

    ⇛   Assign homework.

In one joint session toward the end of our time together, I asked Lauren and Susan what surprised them most about this process, and their answer surprised me. They both said virtually the same thing: "There are people who know how to do this (communicate and manage conflict) because they have a set of skills that can be learned." Lauren and Susan hadn't realized that the ability to manage conflict was about having skills to hold the necessary conversation, and that being in conflict didn't mean they were "bad people." It just meant they needed skills. And now they had them.

Lauren and Susan now had the skills to talk to each other, communicate what was happening, and ask for what they needed without blaming. When we began working together, entertaining how the other person might be feeling or thinking was a faraway notion that sounded like a good idea but nothing Lauren and Susan really wanted to do. The realization that they could—and had—become skilled at these things put smiles on their faces, and mine.

Conduct a Learning Conversation

Faced with the choice between changing one's mind and proving that there is no need to do so, almost everyone gets busy on the proof.
—John Kenneth Galbraith

Most of the time, conflict is set in motion by differing needs, views, values, and/or thinking or behavioral styles. Without experience or training in conflict skills, we often don't know how to ask for what we want, communicate a contrary viewpoint, say no, or express the impact of a coworker's action. When we're unskilled in conflict, we either avoid it or become overly direct and confrontational.

And although we may not have received specific training in conflict and communication, our culture is a powerful teacher. You only have to look around to see how our families and workplaces, schools and unions, corporate and government leaders, friends, neighbors, teachers, and public figures usually deal with conflict and differences. The message? Conflict is a contest that I should stay clear of or win, an unpleasant experience with lasting consequences, or a clash of beliefs that can turn violent. Living in this environment of reactivity, most of us have seen opposing views, frustration, and irritation bottled up or expressed belligerently or positionally—especially in the workplace. Instead of having a dialogue with the person we see as the source of the irritation, we hold back, talk ourselves out of it, or express the frustration to others, creating an unhealthy dynamic that feeds on itself.

In the case of workplace conflict, what the parties need are skills to help them talk to each other and role models who demonstrate learning conversations instead of message-delivery monologues. A learning conversation is exactly that—a conversation in which the primary purpose is to learn:

- How does my partner in the conflict view this situation?
- What am I missing?
- How am I contributing to the conflict?
- What are possible solutions?

Once you learn enough by asking questions, listening, acknowledging, and expressing yourself in this purposeful way, you find a way to solve the problem or, barring resolution, decide how to proceed with respect for each other's differences.

As a coach, your presence and practice with these skills help your employees feel safer discussing what they haven't been able to address in the past as well as show your employees what it looks like to be curious, open, and in an inquiry mode. In aikido fashion, you facilitate the release of this pent-up energy in skilled ways and toward a positive purpose.

The Difficult Conversation

In conflict situations, we're used to witnessing—and often participate in creating—"difficult conversations" instead of "learning conversations." In fact, we are so schooled in that expression that our mindset is programmed to think only of the difficulty we might encounter—not the learning. I'm talking about the conversations we know would be helpful to have, but we leave for another day or, worse, we hold them reactively and ineffectively.

Dozens of well-written, well-researched books, illustrated with compelling real-world examples, have been written about difficult conversations. (You'll find these listed in the Further Resources section at the back of the book.) You may already be familiar with some. If not, I encourage you to choose a title, read it, and decide if you will incorporate its suggestions in your process.

At the same time, we know changing habits requires more than just reading. Real, transformative change of the kind we're talking about happens through experimenting, exploring, and experiencing the benefits—exactly what these individual sessions offer.

As a coach and a participant, I've found it also helps to have a checklist of strategies and practices to refer to. Over the years, in my own research, teaching, and training, I've observed certain best practices that show up time and again. They include:

- Knowing your purpose for the conversation.
- Inquiring, listening, and learning.
- Acknowledging what you're hearing.
- Informing, advocating, and educating.
- Building mutually agreeable solutions.

To simplify these concepts for ease of recall and use, I created the 6-Step Checklist.

The 6-Step Checklist is short enough to remember under stress and blends the central teachings from this extensive field into a list of action items on how to turn a difficult conversation into an exchange of ideas. The 6-Step Checklist Worksheet in Appendix E guides you through the steps in conjunction with a specific conversation.

The 6-Step Checklist

1. **Center.** Prepare for the conversation with centered reflection. Re-center periodically during the conversation.

2. **Purpose.** Clarify your purpose for the conversation.

3. **Inquiry.** Enter with an open and curious mindset. Ask questions to uncover your partner's point of view.

4. **Acknowledgment.** Let your partner know you've heard them.

5. **Advocacy.** Be clear, direct, and respectful in stating your point of view.

6. **Solutions.** Listen for and encourage possible solutions that emerge from the conversation. Follow up.

Steps 1 and 2—Center and Purpose—are the necessary underpinning for any learning conversation and the reason we focused on them exclusively in Chapter 4. Here in Chapter 5, we focus on the three steps that represent the action of the conversation: Inquiry, Acknowledgment, and Advocacy. We look at Step 6, Solutions, in Chapter 7—where we also bring all six steps back together for review, practice, and use in the joint sessions.

In the individual sessions, you're sharing a conflict resolution model and using it to coach the parties through specific conflict scenarios that have stalled the working relationship. In the joint sessions, they'll use the checklist to uncover mutual goals and areas of agreement.

In most difficult conversations, people want to be heard before they listen, which is why we start with inquiry.

Understanding as a Goal

Have you ever dined in a restaurant that has a swinging door in and out of the kitchen? Ever pushed (or watched someone push) on that door when another body is trying to get through from the other direction? What happens? You push, they push, and nobody gets through.

The same push-pushback phenomenon occurs when two people want to get their differing viewpoints across at the same time. It usually sounds something like, "Yes, but you're wrong because . . ." or "No, you weren't listening. What I'm trying to say is . . ." and so on. If you want to get through to the other side and they're not creating an opening, you either let them talk first or push hard enough to get them to hear you. If we extend the metaphor, the more you force, the more they resist. When you push for your way, you virtually guarantee failure because the harder you try to persuade, the harder the opposition will do the same. He wants to be heard just like you.

Inquiry is a powerful skill in your coaching conversations because it helps the parties understand that in order to be heard, they must also be curious, ask questions, and listen. In other words, understanding is the goal—not getting their point across. When they try to understand their conflict partner's view, they create an opening for their partner to do the same. The door swings and they receive their partner's energy, beliefs, and vision, while benefiting from a peek at an alternate reality. They're able to see both views simultaneously while reflecting on how differently their partner perceives the world from the other side of the door. A vivid visual and physical example of this principle is the aikido entry technique known as tenkan. (See the sidebar *Aikido Off the Mat: Tenkan*).

Inquiry

In Step 3, you're helping the parties discover the power of changing their mindset from being certain of a position to being curious and open to learning.

In aikido, when my partner moves toward me, I physically move off the line of attack. This first step protects me. Off the mat, in daily life, I similarly move from certainty to curiosity when I center myself. This inner self-defense move takes me to a new position, where I'm protected. I can view whatever my conflict partner says from a safe place. Their words don't "hit" me in the same way. In more familiar words, I don't take their words personally.

Now that I'm off the line, I can observe where the attack is coming from and where it's going. When I move this way, I can see how to connect with my partner, add my energy to theirs, and guide it to a safe outcome.

Inquiry does the same thing. Asking questions is blending, or adding my energy to theirs. It puts me in the powerful position of learning where my partner is coming from. I hear their intention, hopes, and values. Inquiry also defuses any conflict energy my partner is holding, such as anger and fear, allowing this emotional intensity to find a release valve. Even off the mat, in life, I literally move my body perpendicular to my partner's so I can stay connected to the conversation, while I watch their emotional energy go by and dissipate without affecting me.

Secrets to being in inquiry include:

- ✌ Clearing your mind.

- ✌ Listening with full attention.

- ✌ Making eye contact.

- ✌ When thoughts stray ("I wonder what's for dinner?"), bringing them back to the speaker.

- ✌ Asking questions you don't know the answer to ("What was the most difficult part of that for you?").

- ✌ Helping the speaker reflect on their thinking ("When I offered to help, did it seem like I was being critical?").

- ✌ Proceeding as if you're attempting to solve a puzzle ("What if we tried this?").

- ✌ Pretending you don't know anything about how they see things (you really don't).

- ✌ Trying to understand as much as possible about your partner and their point of view. How do they see the situation? What's the impact of your actions on them? What do they really want for themselves? For this process? For their work?

- ✌ Watching their body language and listening for the unspoken (what are they not saying?).

Teach the parties that what their partner says is how their partner sees things; they're entitled to their view. This reminder helps both parties avoid taking any of the other's comments personally. Help each reframe their partner as a tour guide on a visit to an unfamiliar world. That's how they see it? Fascinating! In this phase of the checklist, both parties are trying to learn as much as possible.

Acknowledgment

Too often we assume that we either have to agree or disagree with the other person. In fact, we can acknowledge the power and importance of the feelings, while disagreeing with the substance of what is being said.
—Douglas Stone, Bruce Patton, and Sheila Heen, *Difficult Conversations*

Acknowledgment is possibly the most underutilized communication skill and the secret sauce that turns difficult conversations into learning conversations. You will forget this. Your employees will forget this. I forget it all the time. But acknowledgment changes the conversation—and the people in it.

Without acknowledgment, all you have is another "Yeah, but . . ." conversation. Even if the parties listen well, if they don't demonstrate that they're trying to understand their partner's meaning and intention, their partner won't feel heard and, consequently, won't be able to listen in return.

Acknowledgment answers three important questions your partner has:

1. "Do you hear me?"

2. "Do you care?"

3. "Are you trying to understand?"

Examples of acknowledging and clarifying statements include:

ↈ "What I hear you saying is . . ."

ↈ "It sounds like . . ."

ↈ "That sounds important. Can you say more?"

ↈ "I'm sorry my action had that impact on you."

- "What specifically would you like me to do differently?"

- "Can you describe what I do or say that makes me appear aggressive (passive, not interested, angry, and so on)?"

- "I'm hearing concern for the project. What areas are you most concerned about?"

- "From what I gather, you're hoping . . ."

- "Thank you for this information."

- "I appreciate your thinking on this."

- "Is there anything else?"

Because acknowledgment demonstrates a willingness and ability to reflect back a view or thought process that is different from—and possibly in opposition to—our own, acknowledgment makes a powerful statement. It says, "I heard you, I'm trying to understand, and this is the meaning I'm making out of what I heard." It shows respect and a disposition toward resolution.

Acknowledgment takes practice. It's not something we see often. In my own difficult conversations, I try to understand my conflict partners well enough to make their case for them. When I can do this, I know I've understood their point of view.

Aikido Off the Mat: Tenkan

Acknowledgment demonstrates respect for my partner's position. In aikido, there's a body movement called "tenkan," most often translated as "convert" or "change." Tenkan "converts" the aikido

attack into energy I can use and is a physical embodiment of acknowledgment.

Imagine you and I are facing each other on the mat. You grab my wrist with both hands and hold on. I can't free myself from the grip. In fact, the more I struggle, the tighter the grip becomes. The wrist grab represents the conflict issue. My arms and your arms correspond to our differing opinions and beliefs, all directed to-

ward the issue. This oppositional stance is how most of us approach conflict—both parties advocating until we're blue in the face. I want you to hear me, and you want me to hear you. And no one is listening.

Tenkan happens in aikido when I pivot from this face-to-face stance to one in which I'm standing side by side with you. When I tenkan, a lot of things change:

- ☙ We're both facing the same direction. I can see what you're seeing.

- ☙ People looking at us would say we're partners rather than opponents.

- ☙ The issue is now positioned in front of our arms (our opinions and beliefs) so we can direct our joint energy toward attacking and solving the problem, instead of attacking each other.

- ☙ It's more difficult for you to hold on to my wrist. When I pivot to your side, there is nothing to fight.

- ☙ Things free up generally.

Verbal acknowledgment of someone else's point of view is like the tenkan. You show you understand the speaker's intention, hopes, and best self.

In aikido, when I tenkan, I align with my partner's energy. Verbal acknowledgment does this, too, and it helps the conversation move toward problem-solving, because it's likely you won't move *off your position until your message is heard. As soon as I pivot from pushing for my way in the conflict to trying to understand and acknowledging what I hear, the conversation lightens. You can unburden yourself of all you need to say. And if I'm successful in listening for understanding, you may eventually reciprocate. In other words, once your message—your position—is acknowledged, you can also move. You no longer have to defend.*

The beauty of it all is that only one of us has to move for things to change for both of us.

Two important aspects of the tenkan metaphor raise frequent questions in my workshops and coaching:

1. ***Why me?*** *Students often ask why it is that they should have to move first. Simply put, the person who has the skill uses the skill. And, in offering this gift, you become a model for others. Waiting for someone without skill to move may take a long time and prolong the conflict. If they don't know how to move into curiosity and acknowledgment, what choice will you make?*

2. ***This feels like manipulation.*** *If it feels like you're listening hard and saying all the right words just to get your partner to do something you want them to do but may not be in their interest, then it's probably manipulation. If, however, you're sincere in your desire to learn from your partner, to see their worldview, and to resolve the conflict, you're practicing inquiry and acknowledgment.*

Contribution Versus Blame

The concept of acknowledgment makes sense. It seems simple, yet it's so infrequently practiced that we have to ask, "How do you teach a person to want to see and acknowledge someone else's point of view?" It's especially challenging when the view seems diametrically opposed, or when one person doesn't like the other, or has decided the other intends harm. It helps if we see the conflict as the result of contributing factors.

In conflict, we're predisposed to blame (making someone else responsible for the problem) and justification (not seeing our own contribution). Falling into this mindset is easy to do and feels good, because I can pretend I'm in the right. The problem, however, is:

- ᴄꜱ Blaming doesn't solve the problem and discounts my contribution to the problem.

- ᴄꜱ When I blame or justify, I give up my ability to influence the other person.

- ᴄꜱ When I give up my ability to influence the other person, I lose power over the outcome.

The concept of contribution solves this dilemma. It isn't them or me; it's both of us, and maybe others as well. What are the contributing factors to this conflict? How has each party helped this situation to evolve? A relevant example is our scenario with Lauren and Susan:

- ᴄꜱ Early on in the conflict, before we started working together, Lauren and Susan were continually annoyed with each other. However, neither person said anything about what was bothering her, preferring to avoid a possible confrontation. They began to blame each other, instead of acknowledging their individual contributions of avoidance and blame.

- ᴄꜱ They each had allies they talked to when they wanted to complain about the problem, which was easier than going to the source. These side conversations contributed to the problem and expanded the negative effects of the conflict to the rest of the office.

- ᴄꜱ Lauren and Susan judged their counterpart negatively, and created a story about her behavior instead of becoming curious and inviting dialogue.

- ᴄꜱ Consequently, Lauren and Susan each behaved according to the story they invented about the other: "Susan refuses to help me, so I'll stop asking" and "Lauren doesn't want help; she'd rather do it alone and get the credit."

There may be external contributing factors as well:

- ᴄꜱ Lauren's and Susan's teammates colluded in the conflict by engaging in gossip with and about them.

     ᆼ Cultural or system norms included managers who wanted to avoid conflict and keep the peace at all costs.

     ᆼ Task-oriented managers applied pressure for the parties to focus on work and not take things personally, but did not help them work on the relationship.

     ᆼ Lauren's and Susan's learning and behavior styles clashed.

Regardless of the reason, the twin traps of blame and justification always lead to more of the same—if we don't know we have other choices.

The good news is that we can use blame and justification as red flags—indications that we're abdicating the only power we really have in conflict. Instead, by choosing to take responsibility for our words and actions, we can change what's not working in the situation and intentionally influence it for the better. In other words, we can notice and change our contribution to the problem. Additional content and applications of the contribution versus blame model can be found in *Difficult Conversations: How to Discuss What Matters Most,* by Douglas Stone, Bruce Patton, and Sheila Heen.

Acknowledgment ≠ Agreement

Another reason it can be hard to acknowledge other people's points of view is that we associate acknowledgment with agreement. The good news is that the parties can learn to keep the two separate. For example, when a speaker says, "This sounds really important to

Acknowledgement ≠ Agreement

you," it doesn't mean the speaker agrees with the statement, only that the speaker hears that the statement is important to their partner.

In other words, acknowledging is not agreement; it's simply repeating back to the speaker what you heard and asking clarifying questions. For example, you can acknowledge but not agree by following up with language such as:

ↅ "I'm not sure I agree, but I'd like to hear more about your point of view."

ↅ "I have a different take on this but would really like to hear why you feel so strongly about it."

Inner Acknowledgment

The parties can also acknowledge their own feelings of anger, annoyance, confusion, and personal defensiveness when they arise.

For me, the process usually starts with an awareness of physical tension—my jaw tightens or I notice I've stopped breathing. In an argument with a coworker over who should take the lead in a training initiative, I said, "Wow, I just got really irritated by that comment, and I think I'm becoming defensive. Can we stop for a moment? I just want to talk about this topic. I'm not trying to persuade you in either direction." The acknowledgment helped both of us to re-center.

Advocacy

The parties in this conflict will need skills to help them say what's on their mind. This is advocacy. When we advocate, we're assertive.

We're saying, "Here's what I see. It may not be how you see it, so I'm going to put the view out there in such a way that you can see it through my eyes."

Advocacy is also standing up for something—a point of view, value, or belief. In conflict, that view can be different from someone else's. It's why conflict is usually conceptualized as a push-pushback archetype, and why inquiry and acknowledgment are such valuable skills.

There are ways to advocate for a position without offending or causing defensiveness. When an individual can advocate in this way, it increases his or her chances of being heard in a conflict. When helping your employees express their viewpoints, needs, and beliefs, certain strategies improve their chances of being heard.

Wait . . .

When advocating a position, it's common to not really listen to what the other person is saying but instead jump in with our perspective too soon. "Yeah, but . . ." is so ingrained in our verbal repertoire it often pops out automatically. If the speaker you're saying that to isn't finished presenting their point of view, they won't hear you. I sometimes play a game with myself to see how long I can wait and how much I can discover about the other person before I begin advocating for my message. It's great practice, and often brings to the surface interesting information and useful insights.

Continue to Clarify Purpose

Remind the parties to continually clarify the purpose of the conversation—their own and that of the other person. What are they really trying to accomplish? Do they want to win the argument, punish their partner, or solve the problem? Focusing on purpose takes participants back to a centered and positive intent.

Don't Assume

It's tempting to assume the other party knows what you're thinking, or that the person should know. Consequently, the parties in your conflict may begin a statement in the middle of a thought without considering whether their partner is aware of their thinking. Remind your employees to tell their side of the story in a way that doesn't make assumptions about what the other person knows or agrees with.

Educate

Because each person's view is unique, your employees need to educate each other on what the world looks like from their window.

Sheila Heen, coauthor of *Difficult Conversations,* tells the story of a car trip with her two-year-old son. He's in his car seat in the back.

When Sheila stops at a traffic light and asks how the traffic light works, her son says, "We go on red and we stop on green, Mommy." He's quite adamant about his view, despite Heen's explanation about how the red-light/green-light system actually works. She's stumped until they arrive at their destination (also at a lighted intersection). She exits the car and goes to the back door to extract her son. Upon leaning in to lift him out of his car seat, she happens to notice that the only view he has is from the side window. He can't see the traffic light in front of the car; he can only see the traffic light on the side street. In his view of the world, we do indeed go on red and stop on green.

Heen's example is simple and poignant. We don't see what they see. They don't see what we see. How can we help each other see through our window? How can we possibly solve a problem without listening for their view and educating them about ours?

Share Facts

Sharing facts is often referred to as the I-Message or I-Statement:

- The Fact ("When you didn't arrive at the agreed-upon time . . .")

- The Feeling (". . . I was concerned.")

- The Hope ("My hope was for your safety and well-being.")

- The Request ("Next time you're going to be late, can you call to let me know?")

A simple assertiveness tool, the I-Message can help both parties share what's happening from their experience without blame or judgment.

The problem is that we often frame "facts" subjectively. "When you ignored me this morning . . ." begins with an interpretation of a situation. The fact may be that the other person innocently walked by without speaking. But we immediately formed an interpretation— "You ignored me"—without realizing it.

Chris Argyris, author, professor, and thought leader in organizational learning, developed a tool called the Ladder of Inference to visually demonstrate how we form interpretations and draw conclusions from available data. At the foot of the ladder lies the data: "You walked by me this morning without speaking." As we move up the ladder, we get further from what actually happened and more deeply into our story of what happened. At the top of the ladder is the conclusion we draw: "You purposely ignored me." Usually, we start the conversation from our conclusion. If I assume you're ignoring me, I can easily draw a conclusion that you will be difficult to work with.

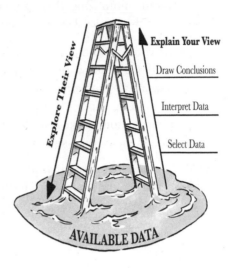

Ladder of Inference

Explore Their View

Explain Your View

Draw Conclusions

Interpret Data

Select Data

AVAILABLE DATA

However, the model also suggests that by being specific about what actually happened—"When you walked by my desk and didn't say anything . . ." —we can climb down the ladder and more accurately describe the data available to us at the time.

Although the Ladder of Inference may seem to be a simple technique, it takes practice to become proficient in using it. And my experience is that the practice delivers untold benefits in helping us grow into more honest, respectful speakers.

As you work with your employees, help them understand that advocating a point of view isn't telling or selling. It's helping someone else stand in our shoes. It's tempting to assume my partner should know what my shoes feel like, especially if I've waited too long to hold the conversation. If I have, I might start by acknowledging that, as in, "I'd like to talk with you about something that's been bothering me. I think this will help us go forward on this project. And I admit, I should have brought this up sooner." This approach also acknowledges my contribution to the problem becoming more entrenched.

After mastering inquiry and the efficient use of questions, the partners in conflict will grow in their ability to address the problem through advocacy because they understand their partner's hopes and needs as well as whether they see the situation in similar or different ways.

In the joint sessions, you will help both parties clarify their needs and hopes without minimizing their partner's. In one joint session that I held, one of the parties was able to advocate in this way:

> From what you've told me, I can see how you came to the conclusion that I'm not a team player. And I think I am. When I point out problems with a project, I'm thinking about its long-term success. I don't mean to be a critic, although perhaps I sound like one. Maybe we can talk about how to address these issues so that my intention is clear?

Notice the aikido metaphor at work—the blending ("From what you've told me, I can see how you came to the conclusion that I'm not a team player") and the redirecting ("And I think I am").

Intent and Impact

When I'm teaching, I talk in terms of intentionality. As we've seen, our intention is almost always positive. We have the best motives, and yet sometimes the intention is received negatively. The impact is not what we intended.

The ability to distinguish between the intent of an action and its impact is useful in learning conversations, and has been helpful in my own practice. In *Difficult Conversations,* Douglas Stone, Bruce Patton, and Sheila Heen note that we often make assumptions and create stories about another's intentions based on the impact their behavior has on us. Usually, we assume the worst. For example, if I feel intimidated, I assume you are trying to intimidate me.

Scenario: You're my teammate, and in a team meeting, you tell me that I missed a key element in creating a new spreadsheet for a project update.

- ✎ Your intent: To help me learn the spreadsheet software and create a positive outcome for the team.

- ✎ The impact on me: I feel inadequate. I see you as critical and trying to look good in front of the team.

A useful strategy is to entertain the possibility that the impact on me might not be what was intended. Imagining a positive intent allows me to field the feedback differently. I can listen with an open mind, take what works, and leave the rest. And, if the delivery was harsh, I can offer feedback of my own.

When you coach the parties in offering feedback, ask them to think about whether their partner is criticizing or trying to be helpful. Being aware that their coworker's intent may be different from its impact, an employee can describe the impact without blaming or becoming defensive. For example:

> Thanks. I appreciate knowing what I missed. And I know your intent was for me to learn the software so we can be successful. Next time you have that kind of feedback, could you give it to me privately?

The aikido metaphor is revealed again in the blending ("I know your intent was for me to learn the software so we can be successful") and redirecting ("Next time you have that kind of feedback, could you give it to me privately?").

Other possible ways to advocate in the spreadsheet scenario might include:

- "Can we talk? When you gave me that feedback about the project spreadsheet, I felt awful. I'm sure it wasn't your intent, but the impact on me is that I felt called out in front of the team. Next time, I'd appreciate it if you came to me privately."

- "In my experience, the content of the spreadsheet is more important than the way it's displayed. Tell me if you see it differently."

- "Do you have a minute? I've been holding on to something that's been bothering me, and I think I've made it worse by not mentioning it when it first happened. Last week, when you said . . ., I took it badly. I thought I'd done a good job, and your remarks were uniformly critical. I'd like to know if you saw anything that was positive."

- "When you stand over my desk, I get nervous. I need time to collect my thoughts. Please let me finish the report, and then we can talk about it."

In each of these examples, the speaker advocates for what they want in a clear, direct, and respectful way.

With this model, you can help your people imagine likely positive motives behind the actions of their coworkers, giving others the benefit of the doubt and making it easier for employees to express themselves and their message.

Finally, knowing the difference between impact and intent helps people lead into an advocacy message with a positive intention. For example:

> When you said you would have the budget ready Tuesday, I took you at your word. My intention is that, as a team, we recognize the importance of deadlines on a project as time sensitive as this. Can you tell me what happened and what we can do to remedy the situation?

In a session with Lauren and Susan, the difference between intent and impact came into our conversation. I learned about a habit that Lauren had developed of not sharing the workload with Susan. This irritated Susan. By not sharing the work, Susan assumed Lauren was micro-managing and dismissing Susan's abilities. Susan grew even more insistent in asking for more work, and it became a point of contention between them. When they learned about the difference between intent and impact, they could talk about what had happened and make sure it wouldn't happen again.

Together we deconstructed the conflict:

Lauren explained her positive intent: She didn't want to give "busywork" to Susan, thinking it was beneath Susan's level of experience.

Susan explained the impact on her: She felt dismissed and ignored. In fact, she was happy to give her best to any work that needed to be done.

Susan asked, "Did you think I was trying to take control (by asking for more work)?"

> *Lauren replied, "No, I never thought you had a negative intention. I'm sorry. I never had a bad intention either (in not giving the work out)."*
>
> *This was a beautiful exchange to watch. And it only took learning a simple yet important skill to express what was happening.*

Model Respect

As people perceive that others don't respect them, the conversation immediately becomes unsafe and dialogue comes to a screeching halt. Why? Because respect is like air. If you take it away, it's all people can think about. The instant people perceive disrespect in the conversation, the interaction is no longer about the original purpose—it is now about defending dignity.
—Kerry Patterson, Joseph Grenny, Ron McMillan, and Al Switzler,
Crucial Conversations

We model respect when we listen for understanding, refrain from making assumptions about others, speak without blame or justification, and recognize that the listener can't know what we're thinking, feeling, or telling ourselves about the world around us. Our view of the world may be—and often is—completely different from theirs. Your employees also have completely different views of the conflict they're in. Respect looks like inquiry, acknowledgment, and advocating in a way that doesn't trample on the right of others to have their own views.

In her book *Teaming,* Harvard professor Amy C. Edmondson explains "naive realism," a phrase coined by psychologist Lee Ross in the 1970s as the human tendency to believe that "I alone am privy to the true reality." In other words, this "invariant, knowable, objective reality" is so obviously true that anyone who doesn't see reality as I do is clearly unreasonable and/or irrational. One outcome of naive realism is that we tend to think everyone believes the way we do, and has similar beliefs and values. Social psychologists call this the false consensus effect. For example, someone might say, "Everyone knows our education system needs serious reform." My sister—an award-winning fifth-grade teacher—might not agree with that statement. And were she to question it, the speaker would perhaps consider her biased, unaware, or worse.

Naive realism and the false consensus effect are about respect or, in this case, disrespect. As a coach, it's important to notice and bring forward when one of the parties makes a statement about a view of reality that their partner may not hold. When the conversation is respectful, both parties feel safe talking about almost anything, and this is the result you want.

If the parties are worried about emotions derailing their best efforts, I find it helpful to redraw my graphic of two concentric circles. This time the smaller circle in the center represents the problem we're trying to solve. The larger outside circle is a safety net that demonstrates positive intent and makes it easier to talk about difficult issues. These practices are foundational for a learning conversation:

- ✌ Curiosity
- ✌ Purpose
- ✌ Centeredness
- ✌ Respect
- ✌ Apology
- ✌ Acknowledgment

In the book *Crucial Conversations,* Grenny, McMillan, and Switzler use a similar diagram that includes a third outer circle containing the words "silence" and "violence." You can help the parties know when a conversation is becoming psychologically unsafe by increasing their ability to notice when one of them shuts down (silence), or becomes sarcastic or demeaning (violence).

When they notice the conversation is moving toward one or the other of these extremes and becoming "difficult," they can bring the conversation back to a "learning" frame by employing one or more of the elements of the outer circle in the diagram—centering, asking helpful questions, listening with curiosity, and reiterating the purpose of the conversation. For example:

> I'm noticing how easy it is to get emotional about this issue, and I'd like to reinforce our purpose—to build a more cohesive work relationship. I'm sorry if I've been talking too much. Please tell me again how you think we could interact more effectively together on this project.

Remember that by using the 6-Step Checklist, your employees are building:

- A readiness to see and acknowledge the other person's humanity and point of view.

- The capacity to manage and express emotional energy purposefully.

- The ability to listen for understanding.

- Skills to turn their opponent into a partner for problem-solving.

In my experience, it usually takes between two and four individual sessions of about an hour each to complete the teaching, application, and transfer of the skills necessary to prepare the parties to meet jointly. The number of sessions depends on how many of the concepts you teach, how well the parties integrate the concepts in their workplace interactions, and how you perceive the parties' readiness and ability to move forward into the joint sessions.

> *In one joint session, Lauren and Susan talked about how their tendencies toward avoidance and judgment caused them to distance themselves in the beginning of their relationship, and how the distancing grew over time. Things such as Lauren's need to*

have all the data before making a decision made her skeptical of Susan's "let's try it and see" approach. And Susan admitted her tendency toward defensiveness often caused her to see Lauren's intention to be helpful as criticism.

To help Lauren and Susan practice addressing their respective blind spots, we created role-plays. In one case, we role-played Lauren offering constructive feedback that could be perceived as critical, so Susan could practice centering, asking useful questions, and looking for Lauren's positive intent.

We also revisited the Ladder of Inference in various workplace scenarios in which Lauren could practice asking for more data, and Susan could practice climbing back down the ladder from defensiveness to curiosity. They each noticed how they moved up the ladder very quickly in conflict.

Practice

1. Role-play. A useful practice in the individual sessions is role-play, or "real play," as a colleague calls it. Choose a few typical difficult interactions and play out conversations using the 6-Step Checklist. You play one role and let your employee play the other. Then switch roles so they can practice both sides.

2. Ask your employee what they think the other person's feelings and needs are around this conflict.

3. Ask your employee to become aware of when their attitude or behavior toward the other party begins to shift.

4. Ask what assumptions they might be making about their partner and invite them to challenge those assumptions.

Before you leave, set a time for the next session. Send a follow-up email with a summary of your notes and suggested homework to be accomplished before the next time you meet. A day or two before the next session, send a reminder email.

We turn now to Phase 3. It's time to bring the parties together. Our purpose in the individual sessions has been to build the parties' skills, confidence, and understanding. As you listened to their stories, you found areas of agreement, confusion, and curiosity, as well as similarities and differences around desired outcomes and expectations.

The quality of being and communication skills you shared have prepared each party to talk to the other in ways they couldn't in the past. And the homework, reading, and self-awareness activities you've engaged in have laid a foundation both parties will use to assemble a new and more resilient relationship.

Homework Examples

- ∾ *Managing Conflict with Power & Presence Workbook:* Review through page 20.

- ∾ Read "Abandon Blame: Map the Contribution System" in *Difficult Conversations.*

- ∾ Read "Create a Learning Conversation" in *Difficult Conversations.*

- ∾ Read "Make It Safe" in *Crucial Conversations.*

- ∾ Look for ways in which you contribute to positive or negative outcomes in the workplace. Bring stories to our next session.

- ∾ Watch for the Ladder of Inference at work in your relationships. Bring examples to the next session.

- ∾ Look for opportunities to interact respectfully, saying "Good morning" and "Thank you," and smiling often.

Key Points

- ∾ Combining a centered presence with key communication strategies helps to change the parties' adversarial dynamic.

- ∾ The 6-Step Checklist offers a succinct summary of best practices for changing a difficult conversation into a learning conversation.

ᏋᎧ Inquiry is an attitude of openness that grounds the conversation in problem-solving and defuses conflict energy.

ᏋᎧ Acknowledgment says, "I heard you, I'm trying to understand, and this is the meaning I'm making out of what I heard." Acknowledgment shows respect and a disposition toward resolution.

ᏋᎧ Acknowledgment moves us from a blame frame to a contribution mindset.

ᏋᎧ Acknowledgment does not equal agreement.

ᏋᎧ Advocacy skills help the parties say what's on their minds, stand up for a value or belief, and help their partner see their point of view.

ᏋᎧ The ability to distinguish between the intent of an action and its impact is a useful tool in advocacy.

ᏋᎧ If the parties have engaged with curiosity, centered intent, respect, and honesty, solutions present themselves.

Sources

ᏋᎧ *Difficult Conversations: How to Discuss What Matters Most* by Douglas Stone, Bruce Patton, and Sheila Heen

ᏋᎧ *Thanks for the Feedback: The Science and Art of Receiving Feedback Well* by Douglas Stone and Sheila Heen

ᏋᎧ *Unlikely Teachers: Finding the Hidden Gifts in Daily Conflict* by Judy Ringer

ᏋᎧ *Crucial Conversations: Tools for Talking When the Stakes Are High* by Kerry Patterson, Joseph Grenny, Ron McMillan, and Al Switzler

ᏋᎧ *Teaming: How Organizations Learn, Innovate, and Compete in the Knowledge Economy* by Amy C. Edmondson

ᏋᎧ *The Fifth Discipline* by Peter M. Senge

PHASE 3
REDIRECTING
(JOINT SESSIONS)

Because of the depth of the connection between us, it only takes one of us to make a change that both of us experience.

6 LOOK FORWARD

If your heart is large enough to envelop your adversaries, you can see right through them and avoid their attacks. And once you envelop them, you will be able to guide them along a path indicated to you by heaven and earth.
—Morihei Ueshiba, founder of aikido

Primary Purpose

Your purpose in the joint sessions is to build rapport, reinforce relationship, and redirect any remaining challenges toward resolution and problem-solving. At this point, we're looking forward to what the rebuilt relationship will look like and how it will be sustained.

Preparation

- Know the purpose and desired outcome for each joint session.
- Consider possible topics for each joint session.
- Read your notes from the previous session.
- Enter with optimism for a positive outcome.

Agenda

- Explain the purpose of the first joint session: to enjoy each other's company and get to know each other apart from the conflict.
- Explain the purpose and goals for subsequent joint sessions.

ℕ Ask for any new developments since the last session.

ℕ Discuss ways to prepare for the next joint session and set a date.

ℕ Take notes and send them in a follow-up email after the session.

ℕ Assign homework.

Jason, Greg, and I were seated at a private table in one of the city's nicest restaurants. We made small talk about the weather, traffic, and the recent holiday. This was our first joint session, and when we were settled in, I reminded them this was an opportunity to share a meal and enjoy each other's company. Our focus for the first session would be topics other than the issues we were working to resolve.

After ordering, the conversation turned to family, and Greg spoke about how much his brother, a local contractor, enjoyed his work. Jason expanded on this theme, sharing his passion for the organization Greg had founded and that Jason now directed, saying it was the perfect job that had everything he looked for in his work—a noble purpose, a stellar staff, an amazing board of directors, and a founder everyone loves. Jason said he woke up looking forward to work every day and, with the exception of the difficulties they were working to resolve, he wouldn't wish for anything to be different. He spoke with passion and conviction.

I could see Greg's surprise. Most of his recent interactions with Jason had not been happy ones. To hear him describe how he loved his work and respected the organization surprised Greg, and he said so. Perhaps for the first time, Greg was seeing a side of Jason he didn't think existed. This was someone Greg had thought of as combative, aloof, and machine-like in his leadership. And yet here was Jason speaking from the heart about his passion and vision for this organization Greg had founded out of love and his own passion.

> *Jason used an analogy of a master carpenter who had built a beautiful house with a solid foundation. He moved into the house and saw some things he wanted to change, but he loved the house and knew it was solid and well built. Greg smiled and said he liked the analogy.*
>
> *After our lunch, a lot changed. There was a "maybe" now. "Maybe" this coaching stuff will work after all. "Maybe" there is more to the story I've created about this person. "Maybe" we can learn to work with instead of against each other.*

The Fun Part!

Here we are at the session many managers want to start with: bringing the parties together to resolve the conflict. And now, the parties are much more likely to make that happen. The joint sessions are a culmination and should be the fun part! Everything you've done up to this point—meeting individually, listening to each person's view of events, teaching skills, and helping your employees gain insight into their contributions—has led to this moment of bringing them together, feeling confident and prepared.

By now, both parties are likely weary of the conflict and ready to find a solution so they can get back to work with a new attitude. Each has a better understanding of the part they played in the conflict, and is eager to try out their new communication skills and mindset. This broader view will help both parties articulate what they've discovered and how they want to work together.

These joint meetings also provide opportunities for each to apologize where appropriate, to listen, and to talk about specific scenarios that have been problematic in the past and ways they will deal with them differently in the future.

If we're looking through the aikido lens, we have aligned and harnessed the parties' energy (through the individual sessions) and are preparing to redirect it toward resolution. As coach, my intention is clear: to help the parties stay safe while guiding any conflict energy toward shared purpose and joint problem-solving. As always: enter, blend, and redirect.

Is It Time?

How do you know when to move from individual to joint sessions? You'll know it's time when the parties seem eager to get on with it, they no longer appear fearful or anxious, and you see them practicing their new centering and communication skills in the workplace. One or two individual sessions may be enough, depending on the severity of the conflict and the parties' motivation to alter the dynamic.

Another gauge is your own sense of optimism. On a scale of 1 to 10, how optimistic are you that the joint meetings will yield a positive outcome; that the parties are ready to resolve their differences and look forward? If you're scoring 7 or higher, I'd say they're ready. And you can always go back to meeting individually.

Build Rapport: First Joint Session

The first of the joint sessions sets the tone for those to come. For that reason, this session deserves special thought and preparation. For example, I suggest you don't move into problem-solving in the first joint session, but rather use the time to build rapport and reinforce relationship. My experience supports holding this session in a neutral location away from the office. I like to take the parties to lunch at a nice restaurant that they'll both enjoy and that offers some privacy. We choose a date, and I ask them to select the restaurant and make a reservation.

Because the primary purpose of this session is to build connection by providing an occasion for the parties to enjoy themselves and talk about topics other than the conflict, I explain we can discuss anything except the problem at hand. I want the parties to get to know each other differently, and the focus to be on interests they have in common (for example, family, food, hobbies, and other topics they like talking about and that reinforce their humanity). You know the parties well enough to help guide the conversation, but try as much as possible to stay in the background.

After we ordered, I asked Susan and Lauren why they'd chosen this restaurant. Susan spoke first and said her family had eaten here for decades. The food was always good, and the staff friendly and efficient. It was their "go-to" place.

Then Lauren related a story about a previous member of the wait staff she happened to know who'd been through some trying and unhappy circumstances. As it turned out, Susan also knew the server well, and her family had helped the same person out of trouble at one point.

This was new information, and the sense of common ground was immediate. Here were two people who both cared deeply about their community and found ways to support those in need.

Topics for the First Joint Meeting

When people talk about what they love, they lighten up. They begin to see each other differently: as human beings with many sides and, oftentimes, common interests. This first meeting is an opportunity to encourage these common interests to surface as well as build trust, respect, and safety. As the coach, you want the conversation to flow and are looking for easy subjects, such as:

- Family
- Movies
- Books
- Sports
- Holidays
- High points and special moments
- Passions and hobbies
- Favorite foods and restaurants
- How both parties came to do this work
- What they like about where they live
- Little known facts they feel like sharing
- A story that best exemplifies what they love about their work

I'm always amazed at how well these first meetings go. There's something about breaking bread together that brings out the best in people. Sometimes we make small talk the entire time, and that's fine. And sometimes an affinity develops and the conversation becomes more informal and personal, as the parties see they have more in common than they thought. This relational ease builds a foundation for future joint sessions and conversations back in the workplace.

Toward the end of the meal, set a date for the next joint session. Explain that it will be a working session in which the three of you will review the process to date and discuss how to apply the parties' new skills to the resolution of the conflict that initiated the coaching. If you offered a behavior or style inventory during the individual sessions, as outlined in Appendix B, ask the parties to review and bring these documents to the next joint session. Also, have both parties bring thoughts about how to proceed, ideas about what they've learned, and suggestions for how these ideas could be useful moving forward, plus any questions or other insights they want to bring to the table.

Practice

Lastly, ask: "What did you appreciate about the luncheon meeting, and how will you bring these qualities into your new workplace relationship?" (Note that you can also use this question to kick off the next joint session.)

Homework Examples

- ೞ Read "Choose to Cocreate" in *The Magic of Conflict*.
- ೞ Review behavior or style inventories (if applicable).
- ೞ Consider the following questions for the next meeting:
  - What skills will you bring to the next session to help facilitate the conversation?
  - What past situations would you like to resolve and how will you contribute to that happening?

- What do you know now that will help you change your working dynamic for the better?
- What questions do you have for your partner or about the coaching process?
- Spend time visualizing how you want your new working relationship to look.

Key Points

ↂ It's time to meet jointly when the parties seem eager to move forward and no longer appear fearful or anxious, and when you see them practicing their new skills in the workplace.

ↂ The primary purpose of the joint sessions is to build rapport, reinforce relationship, and redirect any remaining challenges toward resolution and problem-solving.

ↂ The joint meetings also provide opportunities for each party to apologize where appropriate, to listen, and to talk about specific scenarios that have been problematic in the past and ways to deal with them differently in the future.

ↂ Hold the first joint session in a neutral place (such as a nice restaurant) and focus on what the parties have in common (such as family, food, hobbies, and other topics that reinforce common ground).

Sources

ↂ *The Magic of Conflict* by Thomas Crum

Learning to give and receive energy with each new partner is a challenge and a gift.

7 Resolve, Reflect, Reinforce

Out of clutter, find simplicity. From discord, find harmony. In the middle of difficulty lies opportunity.
—Albert Einstein

Primary Purpose

The purpose of continued joint sessions is to provide openings for the parties to talk about their learning from the individual sessions, compare experiences, and plan for the future. Both parties will explore topics that include:

- What needs to happen for them both to have continued positive engagement?
- What roadblocks may come up?
- How will they resolve future conflict?

Preparation

- Keep the purpose and objectives for the joint sessions in mind.
- Consider your specific goals for this session.
- Read your notes from the previous session.
- Enter with optimism for a positive outcome.

Agenda

- ∽ Ask how things have gone since the last session, and point out positive interactions.
- ∽ Review the purpose and goals, and ask the parties for their thoughts.
- ∽ Review the 6-Step Checklist.
- ∽ Use specific questions to determine what is working and what still needs attention.
- ∽ Discuss behavior or style inventories (if included in the process).
- ∽ Offer the parties an opportunity to express appreciation to each other and for the process.
- ∽ Discuss ways to prepare for the next session and set a date.
- ∽ Take notes and send them in a follow-up email after the session.
- ∽ Assign homework.

In our second joint meeting, Susan said it had been a good week and that communication between her and Lauren was going well. In fact, Lauren had stayed overtime to help her finish a project.

Lauren said she could get centered fairly quickly now. For her, this meant she expressed herself more clearly because she wasn't worried about tripping over her words or wondering, "How will Susan take it?" They both thought one reason the last few weeks had gone so well was because they're not "waiting for something to happen."

I asked if they thought things could revert back to the way they were when the women were in conflict. Lauren said she didn't think so, but if they did, she would go to Susan and talk to her instead of disengaging—her default behavior style.

We talked about some of their assigned reading and where it had been useful. Lauren and Susan said the easiest thing to remember was to center and breathe. In one example from the week before, Lauren told Susan she had "fixed the issue with the file," but Susan said she didn't understand. Lauren stopped, centered herself, and realized she had made the mistake of assuming Susan knew what she was thinking—an old habit that would usually frustrate Susan. Lauren took a breath and said, "Sorry, what I should have said was . . ." and finished setting the context so Susan was on the same page.

I suggested the harmony they were feeling now had been established through:

ભ્ *Hard work*

ભ્ *Skill building*

ભ્ *Replacing ineffective habits with more effective ones*

Susan and Lauren added that they were also using their new skills in many other areas of life—not just this relationship.

Objectives: Resolve, Reflect, Reinforce

Chances are you have gotten off to a great start with your first joint session. Because you built a strong foundation in the individual sessions by listening and aligning with each conflict story—and because the parties now have skills for engaging in learning conversations and problem-solving—the subsequent sessions will fall into place. The players have enhanced their skill sets through individual instruction and practiced them in the workplace. Consequently, they are less fearful and more confident to take the next step in setting their differences aside. At this point, the problem is close to being resolved. In my experience, seldom do you need more than two or three joint meetings. Sometimes one is sufficient (beyond the initial lunch meeting).

As the coach/facilitator, I see the joint meetings accomplishing three overarching objectives, which will be the primary focus of this chapter. If the conversation becomes difficult for any reason, these objectives help me remember what I'm here to do—and what I can't do. I'm here to help the parties:

1. **Resolve** existing challenges by forging solutions that will stand the test of time.

2. **Reflect** on potential challenges and plan ways to deal with them.

3. **Reinforce** their confidence and capacity to handle difficulty in the future.

An important tool in accomplishing them is the 6-Step Checklist, which we'll review here before exploring these objectives in depth.

The 6-Step Checklist: A Review

1. **Center.** Prepare for the conversation with centered reflection. Re-center periodically during the conversation.

2. **Purpose.** Clarify your purpose for the conversation.

3. **Inquiry.** Enter with an open and curious mindset. Ask questions to uncover your partner's point of view.

4. **Acknowledgment.** Let your partner know you've heard them.

5. **Advocacy.** Be clear, direct, and respectful in stating your point of view.

6. **Solutions.** Listen for and encourage possible solutions that emerge from the conversation. Follow up.

At this stage in the process, the checklist is an aid to you and to the parties when you start meeting jointly—whether you engage in one or multiple sessions. Somewhere in this first working session, I remind the parties of the skills they've learned (such as centered presence and new ways to communicate) and invite both parties to practice these skills in our conversations. I ask the parties to relate situations in which they are already using the skills with each other or coworkers. And I emphasize that the six steps are an easy way to recall all we've done together.

As a coach, the six steps keep me on track as well and help the parties see our sessions as a safe practice arena for raising the problems they may face later. I highlight the six steps by referencing them during our conversations, recording them on a flipchart, and asking the parties to reflect on the ones they:

- ∞ Are using most often.

- ∞ Forget most frequently.

- ∞ Want to remember first and foremost.

I urge you to use the six steps as a facilitator's guidepost. The following is a brief recap of the first five steps, plus an exploration of Step 6: Solutions, a primary focus of the joint sessions.

Step 1: Center

When we're centered in the conversation, we help others be centered as well.

As a facilitator, I keep an eye out for uncenteredness from either party. It usually shows up as tension, silence, avoidance, and emotion. I help the parties notice when they've lost their center, so they can choose to return. I usually say something like, "So, I notice a little tension. Does anyone else? That's great. It means we're getting to the heart of the issue. Let's pause for a moment to re-center." I reinforce that when you're centered:

- ∞ Even if words fail, you're still present and can reflect on what you want to ask or say.

- ∞ You can mentally and emotionally step out of the way and let difficult energy go by.

- ∞ You can invite conflict partners to express themselves fully, acknowledge their needs and beliefs, and be ready to express your own when the time comes.

Step 2: Purpose

I always come back to clarity of purpose as the most critical element in the decision to hold a conversation. As their coach, for example, you can reinforce purpose by occasionally asking each person what their reason is for bringing up a challenging issue. Are they trying to justify a past action, or are they offering up the issue as something to solve so that it doesn't happen again? As a coach, you're seeking a well-considered purpose—one that moves the conversation:

- ✍ From "difficult" to "learning"
- ✍ From debate to dialogue
- ✍ From message delivery to problem-solving
- ✍ From dangerous to safe

A purpose one can't control is not useful. For example, they may wish their coworker to be more cooperative, but only the coworker has control of that. However, they can convey that productivity is higher when people are cooperative. Although they can't force the coworker to change, the coworker is likely to be more cooperative because it serves a mutual purpose—a productive workplace. This moves the conversation from "message delivery" to problem-solving.

Other examples of purposes include:

Purposes that Are Not Useful	Purposes that Are Useful
Expecting them to change their behavior for me	Learning why they engage in a specific behavior
Blaming them for what happened	Acknowledging my contribution
Justifying my behavior in an argument	Asking for their thoughts on what happened
Expecting them to agree with me	Expressing my view without expectation of agreement
Thinking, "How can I win?"	Asking, "What can I learn?"

Step 3: Inquiry

Now that the parties are together, encourage them to remember what they learned about the power of inquiry. Suggest examples of open-ended questions they might use to begin talking, such as:

- ❧ "Where would you like to start? What's most important for you?"

- ❧ "Can you tell me what's working and what isn't?"

- ❧ "What else can you tell me about how you see the problem?"

- ❧ "Can you give me one or two ideas that would work for you?"

- ❧ "What's the most difficult part of this for you?"

- ❧ "What's the ideal solution, do you think?"

The questions should invite reflection and seek pieces of the puzzle. This is an empowering gesture for the person asking as well and the person answering. Help the parties understand the importance of maintaining a stance of inquiry, which often appears as patience and waiting for their conflict partner to finish talking.

The last question should always be, "Is there anything else I should know?" The inquiry is finished when the answer is "No."

Step 4: Acknowledgment

Reinforce that it's okay to repeat the speaker's words back to them. Although it may feel foolish to simply parrot the phrase, it isn't. It feels great to hear your words reflected back.

Also, wherever possible, demonstrate acknowledgment as their coach. For example:

- ❧ "From what you're saying, Jamie, you felt exposed when Henry mentioned in the meeting that your project was off target. Is that accurate?"

- ❧ "It sounds like it was really helpful when Pat pitched in to help with the calls."

- ❧ "I'm glad you saw the difference between intent and impact in that situation. That's great!"

Step 5: Advocacy

Remind the parties that advocacy—getting their story heard—often starts with acknowledgment or looking for one thing they have in common with their partner. For example, "John, you've obviously put a lot of thought into this and care a great deal about the outcome. I liked what you said about . . ."

Encourage the parties to think about advocacy as offering information that might be of value to their partner. Advocacy is educating—not selling or manipulating. For example:

> John, from what you're saying, you believe you're doing a good job and living up to the requirements of the job description. I have a slightly different take. As I see it, you put a lot of thought into preparing our meetings and organizing staff, and I think you want to do a good job. I have some ideas about how you can go further, if you choose to, by making a few simple changes. Would you be interested in hearing them?

Step 6: Solutions

With the key elements of communication in place—centered presence, clarity of purpose, inquiry, acknowledgment, and advocacy—the parties are now in a position to see each other and the conflict through new eyes. More important, these key elements prepare them for the last step in the 6-Step Checklist, Building Solutions, a step you will help them with as the joint sessions unfold.

For example, you might notice that a specific problem needs to be solved, such as who answers the phone when both parties are immersed in other tasks, or whose job it is to respond to client requests. Or, it could be a broader problem, such as divergent work styles.

In all cases, if the parties have engaged the process with curiosity, centered intent, respect, and honesty, they also have ideas about possible solutions. If one person makes a suggestion, the other has three ways in which to respond:

1. "I agree."

2. "I agree with what you said with regard to . . ., and I'd like to add . . ."

3. "It seems we have different ideas about how to . . . Can you say more about why you like that approach and how you think it will help us solve the problem in this case?"

In the aikido sense of working with our partner's energy, problem-solving requires listening for energy we can redirect. If Party A proposes a solution that's not perfect, that's still great because something was proposed. Party A gave us energy to work with. Party B should be thinking, "What can I use; what can I add; how can I keep problem-solving as the goal?" Once Party B redirects, they should stay in inquiry and test their solution: "What do you think?" or "Could my idea work?"

As coach, your role is to support the parties by watching how solutions develop. Rather than interrupting the flow of the conversation, take notes you can offer at a later point, if necessary. If things get stuck, suggest a centering pause to let the parties reflect on what they've accomplished so far. Ask them to consider what commonalities they've expressed and how these might come together to solve the problem.

Make sure that plans are made to implement the solutions and ways to follow up are defined. I've seen conversations (some my own) end without actually having an action plan or a solution in place. Both parties listen and talk but walk away from the conversation without articulating next steps and contingencies—a possible recipe for future conflict.

As you look at future scenarios together, encourage the parties to ask and answer questions such as:

- "Where do we go from here?"

- "How will we move ahead together?"

- "What will our working relationship look like after these changes?"

- "How will we hold each other and ourselves accountable?"

At this point, I stand back; I watch the parties as they dialogue and, if need be, I point out things they missed. The less I do now, the more they turn to each other. A partnership begins to form as the parties successfully tackle each potential obstacle and construct a new relationship in the process. In the long run, the solutions that will last are the ones the parties develop themselves; your work is changing from coaching and instruction to observation and support.

If this process uncovers marked differences in values, the checklist becomes even more essential, giving the parties the tools to hold any new challenging conversation respectfully, and with positive purpose and intent. It's possible for people to disagree and still accomplish their purpose of creating a plan to work side by side skillfully, if they employ the six steps.

Powerful Conversation Openings

A common question is, "How do I begin the conversation?" Should the parties need them, the following conversation openers have come from working with organizations, individuals, and my own "off-the-mat" aikido partners. Give the parties a handout and coach them in the use of these openers here and in the workplace:

- ∽ "I have something I'd like to discuss that I think will help us work together more effectively."
- ∽ "I'd like to talk about . . . with you, but first I'd like to get your point of view."
- ∽ "I need your help with what just happened. Do you have a few minutes to talk?"
- ∽ "I need your help with something. Can we talk about it (soon)?" If the person says, "Sure, let me get back to you," follow up.
- ∽ "I think we have different perceptions about . . . I'd like to hear your thinking on this."
- ∽ "I'd like to talk about . . . I think we may have different ideas about how to . . ."

- ᴄ⁄ɔ "I'd like to see if we might reach a better understanding about . . . I really want to hear your feelings about this and share my perspective as well."

Common features in these openers are:

- ᴄ⁄ɔ Letting the other person know up front there will be time for both parties to offer input.

- ᴄ⁄ɔ Being clear this will be a two-way conversation.

- ᴄ⁄ɔ The purpose is a noble one.

Some of these openings use what's known as the mediator's stance. A mediator is able to see a conflict from the point of view of the differences that each party brings to the table. The mediator's stance is a nice, neutral opening that indicates we're not looking for right or wrong, but for how different ideas may be at play and could be helpful in solving the problem.

Logistics

To further support resolution, I think about ways to make the sessions and the room comfortable and conducive to partnering. For example:

- ᴄ⁄ɔ I arrange our seating so the parties are physically aligned and not sitting across from each other.

- ᴄ⁄ɔ As we discuss areas of conflict, I ask the parties to guess and acknowledge what they imagine is the other's point of view.

- ᴄ⁄ɔ Sometimes we set guidelines or ground rules, but not always. It depends on the situation. When I use ground rules, I ask the parties to talk about what would help them feel comfortable holding a problem-solving dialogue, employing the aikido skills we've been practicing, to make the joint sessions a success. The following are the most common requests:

  - Listen and stay curious
  - Seek to understand
  - Know when to take a time out
  - Keep a problem-solving stance

- Maintain a partnering perspective
- Be respectful and kind
- Summarize from time to time
- Pay attention to time

ↄ Review at the end of the session what went well and what to do differently next time

As with everything else, your purpose as well as what you've learned about the parties through the individual sessions will lead you in the right direction.

Resolve, Reflect, Reinforce

Having reviewed the 6-Step Checklist, we now return to our foundational objectives for the joint sessions, which will help keep things on track toward a successful conclusion. These objectives are to:

ↄ **Resolve** any remaining conflicts

ↄ **Reflect** on challenges that may come up post-process

ↄ **Reinforce** the parties' ability to successfully deal with those challenges

Resolve Remaining Conflicts

In their first working session together, I like to seed conversations with questions that invite reflection and dialogue. The questions promote awareness of what's working and where support is still needed. To do this, I usually hand each a sheet of questions and give them time to write down their answers and compare notes. Some examples of questions include:

ↄ "What was your greatest insight?"

ↄ "What is needed to resolve this process so the solution is sustainable?"

ↄ "What are problem areas that could get in the way down the line?"

- ↩ "How will you keep future conflicts from escalating?"

- ↩ "How do you like to receive feedback?"

- ↩ "What are possible difficult situations that may come up, and how will you handle them?"

- ↩ "What's working? Be as specific as you can."

- ↩ "What do you want to keep doing that's working now?"

- ↩ "What's not working?"

- ↩ "What are you concerned about that might cause future conflict?"

- ↩ "What support do you need from each other or someone else?"

- ↩ "What agreements have you made in these meetings about how you're going to handle things differently in the future?"

In addition, I invite the parties to share their experiences about the coaching process and what they've come to appreciate about each other through the individual sessions. For example:

- ↩ "Where were the turning points in the coaching process for you?"

- ↩ "What questions about the process do you have for me or for each other?"

- ↩ "What have you come to appreciate about each other?"

- ↩ "What commonalities have you discovered?"

- ↩ "What differences have you found in your styles that could complement each other?"

- ↩ "What skills or concepts do you want to reinforce?"

- ↩ "How do you want to tell the story of this process five years from now?"

It's also educational to return to the "scale of 1 to 10" questions asked in Chapter 3 or amend them slightly to fit the current conditions. For example:

On a scale of 1 to 10:

- ∾ "How optimistic are you about the conflict staying resolved?"
- ∾ "How would you assess your willingness to resolve future issues together?"
- ∾ "How committed are you to applying the new skills and mindset?"

If the parties completed a behavior or learning style inventory (Appendix B), use this time to talk about what they learned, and invite the parties to compare similarities and differences. For example, if both parties tend to avoid conflict, how have they reframed conflict so they are more likely to address it? If there are different learning styles (for example, attention to detail versus big-picture orientation), we talk about how these styles may have contributed to the original conflict and how this insight can be used to support each other in the future. We create mini-agreements along the way that both parties can carry forward and refer to at work.

In the second joint session, Lauren and Susan talked about what they had learned about themselves through a conflict behavior inventory they'd taken, as well as how they experienced the feedback from their peers and supervisors. Lauren and Susan agreed that some of the peer responses to the instrument were surprising, while others were expected. In general, Lauren and Susan received a good deal of useful feedback, and said it would be nice if all their teammates completed the inventory, so the team could discuss and learn from their different styles.

Lauren and Susan had also completed a more general behavior style inventory, and learned they were both "analyzers." The two women thought this similarity helped explain their respective tendencies toward judgment. In the process of asking each other questions about what pieces of the instrument felt true for them and what they each wanted the other person to know, they found similarities:

> ෨ *Their mutual tendency to withdraw or disengage from conflict caused problems to intensify.*
>
> ෨ *The desire to "get it right" reinforced their inclination toward judgment of each other and themselves.*
>
> *We created role-play scenarios that helped Lauren and Susan practice moving to curiosity and staying engaged in conflict situations.*

Reflect on Potential Challenges

In my teaching and coaching, I toggle between teaching conflict skills and talking about what makes it hard to practice those skills. On the mat, aikidoists practice technique after technique, honing the movements and the flow, trying to embody aikido principles and fundamentals. However, when we're with a challenging partner, often the techniques fall apart. We forget what foot goes where, when to *tenkan,* or how to properly pin our partner. Similarly, in the heat of the conflict moment, at work and at home, we can easily forget to center, breathe, and recall our purpose. That's just the way conflict works and why it has so much to teach us.

In the joint sessions, the task is to reinforce technique and reflect on where the technique might fall apart. I listen carefully for areas of potential future conflict so that we can address these challenges together and decide how the parties will handle them when they arise. It's impossible to predict every problem, but you can reinforce the communication skills in our 6-Step Checklist. This easy-recall model provides support regardless of the conflict:

1. Center

2. Purpose

3. Inquiry

4. Acknowledgement

5. Advocacy

6. Solutions

Similarly, the simple self-command to stop, center, and breathe is often all that's needed to regain composure and choice. Those you are coaching need to leave the process knowing the first thing they will do when feeling trapped, regardless of the nature of the trap. Each should have their "reset button." And it's important they do. Some examples include:

- ✑ "I'll notice, step back, and center myself."
- ✑ "I'll remember to be curious and ask a question."
- ✑ "I'll stay present and listen first."

Reinforce Ability and Commitment

At some point, this process will conclude and the parties will be left to their own resources; you can't be with them all the time. And if you're using an outside consultant, they'll eventually leave as well. Once back in the workplace, you want the parties to feel confident and capable when they encounter the next dilemma. I'm often asked, "Who will play your role when you're not there? Who will have the foresight to say, 'Wait, let's take a moment to think and decide how to handle this.' Or, 'Can we talk about what just happened?'"

Ideally, when the joint sessions are complete, each of the individuals will be able to do this for themselves and for each other. They'll have the necessary confidence and ability to notice conflict developing and take steps to change direction. To that end, you want to take every opportunity during the joint sessions to notice the positive choices they're making and point them out. I try to spot topics where the parties are aligned, draw attention to areas of agreement and commonality, and acknowledge skill. I suggest you do the same—look for what's working and reinforce it, as in:

- ✑ "Wow, nice job paraphrasing that comment!"
- ✑ "I appreciate how you took a moment before you answered. You appeared to be reflecting on what you heard and deciding how to respond."
- ✑ "That was a well-phrased question. You're really understanding the power of inquiry, aren't you?"

Also, watch for moments when the parties seem unprepared or anxious, identify the problem if there is one, and ask what tool from the repertoire would help resolve it—always looking for what's working and appreciating it.

You want to continually be thinking, modeling, and reinforcing: "You can do this!"

If you hold multiple joint sessions to resolve different areas of conflict, encourage the parties to guess at each other's viewpoint in each case, and acknowledge each other's contributions and positive intent. Use questions from "Resolve Remaining Conflicts" on page 148 to stimulate further conversation about values, wisdom gained from this process, and what a sustainable resolution looks like.

Lastly, if you choose, the parties can complete a written document cataloging their learnings and accomplishments. For this, we turn now to Phase 4: Bowing Out, during which we'll look at ways to follow up as the process comes to a close.

Practice/Homework Examples

- ∞ Choose one skill or concept to focus on, and bring stories about how you used it to the next session.

- ∞ Write an opening for a learning conversation you'd like to have with someone and bring it to the next session.

- ∞ Bring questions for your partner or about the coaching process in general.

- ∞ Notice how you contribute to the relationship this week.

- ∞ Keep notes of situations that might have been problematic in the past and how you responded.

- ∞ Think about what you would like included in the joint agreement (if you choose this option).

Key Points

- ∞ The purpose of continued joint sessions is to provide openings for the parties to talk about the individual sessions, compare experiences, and plan for the future.

- Objectives for these sessions include resolving existing challenges, reflecting on potential challenges, and reinforcing confidence and capacity to handle future difficulty.

- The 6-Step Checklist is a foundational framework for the joint sessions.

- Useful conversation openers let the other person know there will be time for everyone to offer input.

- It's important to come to the joint sessions prepared with questions that invite the parties to reflect on their experiences, ask questions of each other, and offer feedback.

- When the joint sessions are complete, each of the individuals will acknowledge areas of alignment, agreement, and commonality.

- They will also identify areas of potential future conflict, and decide how to handle them should they arise.

- Reinforcing skills and positive choices you're observing will support the parties as the process concludes.

Sources

- *Difficult Conversations: How to Discuss What Matters Most* by Douglas Stone, Bruce Patton, and Sheila Heen

PHASE 4
BOWING OUT

Conflict is a restriction of energy. Your task is to free up that energy for more productive and purposeful use—for your people, your team, and your organization or company.

8 REVIEW AND FOLLOW-UP

Those managers who thrive and who look forward to coming to work every day are those who proactively, respectfully, and thoughtfully address conflict rather than those who seek to ignore it or pass it on to another manager or department. The question is not whether you are a conflict manager. The question is, "What kind of conflict manager are you?"
—Susan S. Raines, *Conflict Management for Managers*

The energy of our differences can produce a precious gift we could never have experienced without them.
—Thomas Crum, *The Magic of Conflict*

Primary Purpose

The primary purpose is to establish a review process to make sure the new habits and relationship are holding, as well as to design a support system for the future.

Preparation

- ✧ Know your purpose.
- ✧ Read your notes from the previous session.
- ✧ Enter with optimism for a positive outcome.

Agenda

- ✧ Ask for any new developments since the last session.
- ✧ Decide whether the parties will write an agreement and what system of follow-up you'll use.

- Talk with the parties' manager(s) (if this isn't you) to help decide how much and what kind of follow-up is necessary.

- Agree on how much transparency you will employ with other members of the team.

- Take notes and send them in a follow-up email after the session.

New Life at Work

At the end of an aikido class, we bow to each partner we practiced with. We do this quietly from a seated position, called "seiza." Then we bow as we leave the mat, also from seiza. We make a final standing

bow as we exit the space. We bow a lot—to our partners, to our instructors, and to the space. In aikido, as the saying goes, "When in doubt, bow!"

Aikido etiquette revolves around the bow, which represents respect and gratitude. Bowing in

and out are ritualized traditions in dojos around the world. When we bow in, we're saying, "I'm ready to learn, I'm fully present, and I'm willing to practice and take on all that goes with it. I'm willing to try, fail, try again, and eventually reach a new level of skill."

When we bow out, we're saying, "Thank you very much for this opportunity to practice these techniques and to learn with you and from our teachers."

Most aikidoists leave the dojo intending to use not just the martial techniques, should the need arise, but to utilize the principles of entering, blending, and redirecting in their daily lives as well. Aikidoists enter the practice as beginners, and gradually gain skill and experience. The way of aikido starts to feel more and more familiar as the days, months, and years go by.

In a similar way, although the skills to manage conflict are not always intuitive or obvious in the workplace, they exist and can be learned. We weren't born knowing these skills, and in many cases, have learned conflict habits that are not productive or helpful. However, we change ineffectual habits by adopting new ones that serve us more intentionally, and we become proficient by practicing them. Adopting and practicing new habits is what this book is about.

You've been engaged in a phased intervention that has reached a successful conclusion. You and your employees, partners, or coworkers have all learned from the process, and are better prepared to deal with conflict at work and elsewhere. You're bowing out, but you're not leaving. As an internal manager or supervisor, you continue to witness the day-to-day interactions of the people you've been coaching, and you remain an influence as you return to your former role in their work lives. Unlike my external consultant responsibility, which disappears when I bow out, your responsibility and challenge will be to act as if you've disappeared, so your employees can practice working through any future difficulties on their own. You'll be there if needed, and you'll check in periodically.

Writing an Agreement

If a letter of agreement is part of the process, it shouldn't be a surprise or left to the final session. When I'm asked to include this agreement, I let the parties know at the outset and ask them to take notes along the way about what goes into that agreement. If, during the coaching process, the parties choose to create an agreement, the same applies. I take careful notes and ask them to keep their own notes to use later.

Usually, the document is fairly simple. It states specific behaviors the parties are requesting from each other; how they intend to address future setbacks; how to request support from management; and, sometimes, consequences if the parties don't fulfill the agreement. In my own session notes, I circle topics that I think should go into the agreement and bring them up if the participants forget. When it's time to create the document, I ask for their thoughts and record them on a flipchart. I use questions similar to those listed in Chapter 7. For example:

   ❧ "What do you want to keep doing that's working now?"

   ❧ "What are possible difficult situations that my come up, and how will you handle them?"

   ❧ "How will you keep future conflicts from escalating?"

   ❧ "How do you like to receive feedback from each other?"

   ❧ "What support do you need from each other or someone else?"

   ❧ "What agreements have you made in these meetings about how you're going to handle things differently in the future?"

If I see something in my notes that is not brought up by the parties, I offer it for inclusion. When all our thoughts and requests are up on the flipchart, we create a written agreement. I often have them write it up themselves.

I find creating an agreement together to be one of the more rewarding aspects of finalizing the process; I enjoy watching the parties work together to shape what their future work relationship will look like. A sample agreement is included in Appendix F.

Including Others in the Process

Although the intervention is closing for the parties involved, others on the team or in the organization may have been aware of the ongoing coaching sessions. Coworkers and others affected by the original conflict may have also noticed the changes in the parties as they progressed. And even when the coaching goes well, there may be residue left behind from the original conflict. How do you let the larger group know the issue is resolved? Do you want to be transparent about the process?

If you haven't already, now is a good time to talk to the parties about whether and how they would like to include the rest of their team, department, or organization in the process. Over the years, my clients have taken different approaches, and usually the parties—in conjunction with their manager or HR professional—decide together on this step. Sometimes, due to confidentiality requirements, nothing at all is said. If the parties decide they want to involve others, the method can be as simple as a few personal conversations, an email, or a presentation at a team meeting.

In my work with Susan and Lauren, in addition to talking with their peers, Susan wrote an article for the company newsletter sharing her experience, and explaining the benefits of studying conflict and communication skills. Although Susan and Lauren began the process as skeptics, they learned how practicing a few simple skills gave them the personal power to deal with conflict and difficult communication in all areas of life.

These women accomplished much more than the resolution of a conflict. They became spirited leaders and skilled role models for their team and organization. This is not unusual. In my experience, people are empowered by the skills in a way that makes the parties want to share their new perspective on how conflict and difficult communication can be skillfully managed.

Follow Up and Check In

At your final joint session, you decide together what follow-up looks like. How will you, as their manager, check in with the parties to make sure they feel confident about the post-process relationship, and supported in using their new skills and principles? Do you want to wait a period of time (possibly sixty to ninety days) or would you prefer to have more frequent check-ins? Do the parties want a more formal meeting to discuss what's working and what needs work, or do you all prefer a more informal approach? Is there a format somewhere in between? There are no right answers; what you decide together is the solution you implement.

Annie, my VP of HR colleague, prefers an informal approach: checking in with one party, then the other—always in the same week. Instead of an office meeting, she and her people are spontaneous. She makes it a point to meet first with their manager or supervisor to see if the manager's recounting of events matches the employees'. Sometimes the employee is more interested in sidestepping a new problem or in presenting a good front. Depending on what the manager says, Annie either follows up or leaves well enough alone.

Annie's follow-ups may find her running into one of the parties and casually asking, "How's it going? Everything okay?" Depending on the response—"Well, um, okay, I guess" or "Great! Things are really good"—Annie knows whether more follow-up is needed. In general, she stays alert to how the parties are getting along and occasionally slips in a wake-up call, when/if needed. According to Annie, "It's important to know when to let things go and when to intervene. You don't want to appear aloof, and you don't want to keep poking at a conflict that's been resolved."

Another HR director colleague takes a more formal approach, meeting once a month for about a year to continue the conversation with questions such as:

- "What do we want?"
- "What do we need more of?"
- "What's working?"
- "What are the current challenges?"
- "What are the solutions?"

The employees offer input, my colleague offers her observations, and they decide when to meet again.

A third option is one sixty-day follow-up. A manager I know in a highly competitive tech company likes this approach because the parties know they will be held accountable at that meeting for their actions during the last sixty days. He sends an email prior to the meeting with a few questions similar to the ones above for the parties to reflect on and discuss at the meeting.

One pair of coworkers enjoyed the regular opportunities to talk together so much they created their own follow-up system. In addition to a sixty-day meeting with their manager, the two decided to meet on their own, off campus, for lunch and a relationship check-in each month for a year.

Three Possible Outcomes

All the parties in this intervention have worked hard, and learned a lot about how to resolve conflict, hold learning conversations, and practice centered presence, personal power, and clarity of purpose. However you decide to follow up, ideally the meetings are little more than a pat on the back for all involved. And, because conflict exists, there will be setbacks and opportunities for continued practice.

Generally, assuming the parties continue in their current positions, there are three possible outcomes to the intervention:

1. **The conflict is resolved.** The parties walk away with new skills, the manager is pleased, and things go forward with energy and effectiveness. Your people have increased awareness and a healthier relationship. Barriers have dropped, attitudes are lightened, and life at work is generally more effortless and definitely less stressful for everyone involved.

2. **The conflict is not resolved.** Preferably, you'll know early in the process whether either or both parties are unwilling or unable to make the necessary changes, or if the conflict has progressed in a way that makes resolution unlikely. You may foresee this during the individual sessions, decide to stop the process, and go to Plan B: performance review, transfer to another position, or termination. If you find yourself in this situation later on during the joint sessions, you will do the same—stop the process, share your observations with the individuals (and their managers), and decide how to proceed. It will help if you've thought about such a contingency at the outset.

3. **The conflict seems resolved.** The parties work together well for a while, but in time, the working relationship deteriorates and falls back to where it was at the beginning. If you have an agreement and there are consequences or contingencies built into the agreement, you'll know what to do. If the parties did not create a written agreement and consequences have not otherwise been defined, I suggest meeting individually again to see what was missed, how things got off track, and whether the parties are willing to try again. At this point, make a decision about continuing with a joint meeting or employing Plan B.

In my experience, you almost always know in the first one or two individual sessions whether the process will be successful. Trust your instinct. Don't be afraid early on to tackle the hard questions. Ask yourself whether, knowing what you know, working with these people is worth your investment of time and energy. When your answer is "Yes" and your goal is to support their process, you will find the road that takes you where you want to go.

Key Points

- It is important to establish a system of review to make sure the new habits and relationship are holding and to offer support when needed.

- At your final joint session, decide with the parties what follow-up will look like—formal or informal, and how often.

- Decide if the parties will write an agreement and how they will address future setbacks.

- Agree on whether and how you will be transparent about the process with other members of the team or organization.

- If the working relationship deteriorates after the coaching is over, consider meeting again.

- It helps to have an agreement in place in the event the dysfunction continues.

- If you have an agreement and there are consequences or contingencies built in, you will know what to do.

Vibrant and Joyful

My purpose in writing this book has been to help you be successful in supporting your people to communicate, resolve their differences, and work together amicably and productively. Conflict is a restriction of energy. Your task is to free up that energy for more productive and purposeful use—for your people, your team, and your organization or company. Imagine untangling a knot. You go at it slowly and methodically. You stay focused and present, seeing how each strand plays a part in the restriction and where the knot is most unyielding. You work gently in order to find where the strands want to move. You don't push or pull; you work with them, guiding them until the strands are free to move independently to accomplish their purpose.

Aikido's founder, Morihei Ueshiba, wrote, "Always practice the Art of Peace in a vibrant and joyful manner." This principle underlies all of my work. I offer it to you. When you engage in this process, you are practicing the Art of Peace.

Bow in.
Enter, blend, redirect.
Bow out.
Practice, practice, practice.

I wish you good ki on your journey!

Appendix A
Before Action Review

I hope you find the following questions helpful as you consider whether and how to begin your coaching intervention.

1. What's my intention?

- ✑ Description of the conflict and employees involved
- ✑ Purpose/desired outcomes
  - · For myself
  - · For the parties
  - · For the organization
- ✑ Mindset for maximum benefit (my attitude going in)

2. What would success look like?

- ✑ Benefits of resolving the conflict
- ✑ Vision of the future with conflict resolved

3. What will some challenges be?

- ✑ In what areas might I encounter difficulty?

- Internal and external challenges and limits

  - What personal habits, judgments, or tendencies could interfere?

  - What external pressures are present?

- Costs/benefits of continuing the status quo
- Alternatives to a successful resolution of the conflict

4. What do I know from past experience?

- What have I learned from other situations like this?

  - My own experiences

  - Others' experiences

- What makes me think I will be helpful here?

5. What will increase the likelihood of success this time?

- What people, reference material, and personal strengths will support me in the process?
- How will I handle the unexpected?

6. When will I review accomplishments?

- What is the time frame I'm anticipating?
- How and when will I write about the process?

Appendix B
Style Instruments

The individual sessions are an opening for the parties to get to know their unique styles of behavior, learning, and conflict, as well as how these styles support or hinder their workplace dynamic. There are numerous online and printed self-assessment instruments, also referred to as profiles or inventories, which allow the individual to see their tendencies, trigger points, and reactive style under stress. Most can be given as individual profiles or as a 360-degree assessment, which has the advantage of showing not only how the taker perceives their style but also how others experience the taker's style when it interacts with their own.

Having each party complete one or more of these assessments offers insight that enriches the conversation and learning during the individual sessions. In the joint sessions, I invite the parties to compare results, talk about similarities and differences in style, and generate theories about how their different styles may have contributed to the conflict.

These instruments can be revelatory in demonstrating how different ways of viewing the world impact a relationship. For example, an introvert could be seen as unfeeling, arrogant, or unintelligent to an extravert. Similarly, an accommodating conflict style is less likely to express their point of view and might wait too long to bring up problems. When the parties see how their different (or similar) styles have been acted out in the workplace, they can view the conflict from a more objective place.

I've found the following style indicators to be helpful in generating learning conversations:

The Thomas Kilmann Conflict Mode Instrument (TKI)

Used primarily as an individual assessment, the TKI reflects the taker's tendencies in five conflict styles: avoidance, competition, compromise, accommodation, or collaboration. You see the strengths and drawbacks of each style and the circumstances where each style is helpful or unhelpful.

    ∾ *https://www.cpp.com*

The DiSC Personality Assessment

A commonly used assessment in teambuilding and communication training, this instrument measures tendencies toward certain behaviors. The DiSC letters stand for Dominance, Influence, Steadiness, and Conscientiousness, and show how the individual taking the assessment relates to others.

    ∾ Everything DISC, *http://www.everythingdisc.com*

As I See Myself

Offered by Effectiveness Institute, "As I See Myself" is a twenty-one-page booklet that reveals the taker's behavior style and summarizes the associated strengths and challenges for that style. "As I See Myself" is designed as an individual style instrument and can also be used in conjunction with "As Others See Me," in which case, the taker receives feedback from others on their style.

    ∾ Effectiveness Institute, *http://www.effectivenessinstitute.com*

Myers-Briggs Type Indicator® (MBTI®)

Historically used in organizational teambuilding, interviewing, and coaching, the Myers-Briggs Type Indicator identifies, measures, and describes where the taker's basic preferences fall among sixteen distinctive personality types. The taker will find out, for example, if they are more extraverted or introverted, sensing or intuitive, a thinker or a feeler, and whether they prefer to get things decided or to stay open to new information. The MBTI requires special training to administer and help the taker to fully understand the results.

    ∽ The Myers-Briggs Company, *https://www.themeyersbriggs.com*

The Conflict Dynamics Profile

Specifically created to measure constructive and destructive behaviors in conflict settings, the CDP also measures hot buttons that trigger emotions. Examples of constructive behaviors are reaching out, reflective thinking, and expressing emotions. Some of the destructive behaviors measured by the CDP are retaliating, demeaning, and avoiding. Taken as a 360-degree instrument, it helps the taker see discrepancies between how they rate themselves on constructive/destructive scales and how others—peers, direct reports, and their supervisor—perceive their behaviors. The CDP requires training to administer and help the taker to fully understand the results.

    ∽ Conflict Dynamics Profile, *http://www.conflictdynamics.org*

APPENDIX C
TURN ENEMIES INTO ALLIES "LITE"

An early reader reflected that following the process as outlined in this book could be time intensive. That's true. The kind of conflict we're talking about is seldom resolved quickly, especially if it evolved over time. The unraveling also deserves time and attention.

She also asked me how readers would know when to engage in a full-fledged version of the process, when they might apply a "lite" version, and what "lite" might look like.

The idea of a "lite" model made me smile, and I think she was spot on in asking the question. However, there are certain parameters. For example, if the conflict is entrenched, then I say dig in and take the time necessary to fully explore and sort it through.

On the other hand, a "lite" version of the four-phase model might be appropriate if:

- ◈ You're working with individuals who are already highly skilled and are just not applying their knowledge and awareness with each other.

- ◈ Past experience gives you confidence about your ability to manage an intervention like this and you only need a few suggestions.

- ◈ You have rapport and a history of prior success with the parties involved.

In these cases, you can keep the sessions to a minimum and still follow the four phases:

Phase 1: Working on Yourself Alone

Do a personal tally before you begin. Include:

- **Mindset:** Are you optimistic about the outcome? Can you communicate that optimism to the parties?

- **Purpose:** What are you hoping for as an outcome: for the parties involved, for yourself, and for the team or organization? What will change if the intervention is successful?

- **Quality of Being:** Will you be able to maintain centered presence, personal power, and clarity of purpose despite possible setbacks?

- **Non-Judgment:** How do you feel about the parties, and can you adopt an attitude of non-judgment, appreciation, and curiosity toward them?

- **Support:** Will you be able to refrain from trying to solve the problem yourself in favor of helping them forge their own solutions?

- **Curiosity:** What do you need to know going into the process?

Phase 1 is key to understanding and establishing the foundation for your work. If you enter the coaching sessions with centered presence, personal power, and clarity of purpose, you're most of the way to a successful end. Reading the Introduction and Chapters 1 and 2 will ground the qualities most helpful to you as coach and facilitator of the process.

Phase 2: Individual Sessions

One individual session with each of the parties may be enough if they are aware of their part in the problem and are willing to commit to working to resolve it. You will want to hear from each about:

ᴄᴠ᎒ Their view of what the conflict is about, including their own contribution.

ᴄᴠ᎒ How they imagine the other party is thinking and feeling about the conflict.

ᴄᴠ᎒ What they think needs to happen to resolve it, and how they will play a part in the resolution.

ᴄᴠ᎒ What they think the other party needs in order to resolve the conflict.

ᴄᴠ᎒ Possible consequences for not resolving the conflict.

ᴄᴠ᎒ The ideal outcome as they see it.

ᴄᴠ᎒ Skills they will bring to bear at a joint meeting to resolve the conflict.

Don't invite the parties into a joint session until they're ready. Ask them if they think they are. Role-play possible scenarios, taking on different parts so they can practice being themselves but also take on their conflict partner's role. Trust your intuition and don't move into joint problem-solving too soon. If you bring them together before they're ready, it may make the situation worse.

Phase 3: Joint Sessions

One joint session may also be appropriate if you get a positive feeling from the individual sessions, and if you see the parties as having a common purpose to resolve the conflict and work together more effectively going forward.

If, during the joint session, the parties begin to rehash past slights or old conflict, redirect them toward the future. Help them move away from conversation about what caused the conflict to how they will behave differently in the future so that it doesn't happen again. Review Chapters 4 and 5 on Personal Power and Communication Strategies, and don't hesitate to go back to individual sessions, if needed, to teach and role-play the skills they're not using.

There should be time in the joint sessions for:

- ∾ **Building rapport:** Start with small talk—the weather, sports, happy events at work, family news, and other topics that reinforce common ground.

- ∾ **Appreciation:** Generate questions about what they appreciate about each other's work ethic, behavior, attitude, or general workplace demeanor.

- ∾ **Reflection and requests:** Ask what each will do differently to ensure a smooth transition from the conflict into a more cooperative workplace relationship.

- ∾ **Contingency planning:** Explore specific scenarios they will approach in new ways.

- ∾ **Apology:** Invite each party to consider what they can sincerely say they're sorry for.

- ∾ **Reinforcement:** Make time to acknowledge what each of you appreciate and want to reinforce about how the parties engaged the process.

- ∾ **Resolution:** Gain agreement on what the parties are committing to, and how they will hold themselves accountable.

Phase 4: Review and Follow-Up

Before you close the last joint session, establish a system of follow-up, review, and support. Decide together how you will check in with them. Possibilities include:

- ∾ A formal follow-up, as in another joint meeting in sixty to ninety days.

- ∾ Informal and spontaneous, as in, "How are things going?"

- ∾ Periodic email follow-up.

Determine how you'll know when follow-up is no longer required, as well as what to do if the relationship begins to revert to old patterns.

If you think a "lite" version is appropriate to your situation, by all means, give it a go. You'll know soon if more is required. The initial meeting as outlined in Chapter 3 should be helpful.

SUPPORT BETWEEN SESSIONS

The following are samples of the type of homework assignments and notes I send by email directly following a session—usually the same day or within twenty-four hours. The purpose is to create an environment of continuous learning and practice. I want the parties thinking about the concepts and practicing the skills day to day, not only during the sessions.

The following notes are partial and for sample purposes only, and are examples of the content arising from my observations during the sessions.

Based on what I see and hear, I assign homework to reinforce the instruction and engage the parties in the learning process. In addition, this follow-up process lets them know they've been heard, correct any misunderstandings, and spot recurring patterns.

Samples from Individual Sessions

Individual Follow-up Email—Session 1

Hi (name),

Thank you for your time, enthusiasm, receptivity, and willingness to jump into this work. I really enjoyed our session today and look forward to next time—May 15, 9 a.m., at (location).

Notes and homework are listed in the email. If I missed an important moment, please let me know.

Thank you, (name) Please confirm receipt. And have a great week!

Homework

- ⟳ Read through Chapter 6 in *Unlikely Teachers.*
- ⟳ *Managing Conflict with Power & Presence Workbook:* Review through page 10.
- ⟳ Come to the next session with at least three things you admire or respect about (conflict partner's name).
- ⟳ Look for opportunities to practice centering and notice what happens. Bring stories about centering to the next session.
- ⟳ Keep a conflict journal and bring it to the next session.
- ⟳ Begin meditation practice as outlined during the session.
- ⟳ Establish a routine of getting out of your office space for ten to fifteen minutes twice a day, in order to de-stress and regain perspective.
- ⟳ In the *CDP Development Guide,* read the page on Reflective Thinking and do the first two development activities.
- ⟳ Watch two videos on *The Power of Habit* by Charles Duhigg
    - Random House, "How to Break Habits" from *The Power of Habit* by Charles Duhigg, *https://www.you tube.com/watch?v=W1eYrhGeffc*
    - Epipheo, "The Power of Habit," *https://www.youtube. com/watch?v=wQLHwSphu-M*

Notes

൭ You read the Introduction to *Unlikely Teachers* and appreciated the aikido metaphor.

- The idea of "conflict as opportunity" resonated; you'd "like to operate that way."

- You also like the idea of choosing a centered response under pressure—the ability to be calm and in control.

൭ You have high expectations of yourself and others.

൭ When I asked about your purpose for our work together, you said you would like to communicate more effectively with (name). You also want to resolve the ongoing issues and "put this episode behind you."

൭ We did an aikido exercise called *Moving from Resistance to Connection*.

- You quickly applied the metaphor, saying it was about combining energies and working toward the same goal.

- It was a different way to look at conflict.

൭ We had a conversation about sarcasm. You said this trait runs in your family, and it can be a way to feel like you belong.

- You noted that everyone doesn't receive sarcasm the same way. For you, it feels like you're connecting, but for others it can feel hurtful or disrespectful.

൭ We practiced a centering exercise, and it reminded you of how you feel when you're running.

൭ We practiced the *Unbendable Arm* exercise.

- For you the third arm—the energy arm—was about the ability to focus on the purpose of the conversation and not get distracted by tangents.

· We also talked about emotions, and that centering is not about suppressing emotion but rather a container that allows us to witness emotional energy and decide how to use it in a more constructive way.

· The first arm = aggressive behavior, words, actions.

· The second arm = passive or passive-aggressive.

· The third arm = assertive, purposeful, direct, respectful.

Individual Follow-up Email—Session 2

Hi (name),

Great work today. Thank you for your perseverance in the pursuit of a goal. I'm talking about our common goal of finding your highest, most centered and capable self. Watching you find your centered presence in our role-plays and seeing you jump into Discovery by choosing a curious state of mind was personally rewarding. Not everyone can do that at will. It's one of the primary indicators of awareness and compassion for self and others. Bravo.

I look forward to next week, and will be eager to hear if you have the conversation we practiced and how you found your center in it.

Meanwhile, homework and notes . . .

Homework

ᴄ⃜ Continue journaling and meditation.

ᴄ⃜ Finish reading *Difficult Conversations.*

ᴄ⃜ Please read the attached HBR article, and let me know if/how it helped with your upcoming conversation.

ᴄ⃜ Brainstorm questions for our joint sessions.

℥ Think about your interactions with (name) and how you will apply the 6-Step Checklist in your upcoming conversation.

℥ Watch for examples of people jumping up the Ladder of Inference (yours and others). Bring examples to the next session.

Notes

℥ Your conversation with (name) went well. You feel like a weight has been lifted.

℥ When I asked about your thoughts on progress in general, you said:

- The books, behavior style profile, centering, gaining skills, and having tools you never had before were helping you learn new things that were good for a lot of areas of life, not only this specific relationship.

℥ We took a look at your Conflict Dynamics Profile assessment.

- You recognized Yielding as something you do a lot, which hasn't been helpful with (name).

- Your primary hot button is Micromanaging. Someone who pushes this button is (name), as well as some members of your family.

℥ When we started brainstorming behaviors that others might label retaliatory, we came up with:

- The conversation you had when you said you were resigning.

- The fact that some people see retaliation in behaviors like shutting down or avoiding.

℥ We went through the CDP Development Guide and worked on Approachability as a Dynamic Goal.

    ℥   You and (name) are more aligned, and more trusting of each other.

    ℥   You are rebuilding rapport, and the two of you have work-related conversations more easily.

Samples from Joint Sessions

First Joint Session Follow-up

Follow-up email

Thank you for our lunch session today. I hope you enjoyed it as much as I did. I think you know each other pretty well, although I hope a few new insights were gained. It can be interesting and fun to get to know someone beyond their role at work.

I look forward to next week and our first working session together. Please plan on ninety minutes. Between now and then, review what you know about the following concepts we've covered in our individual sessions, so that we can talk about how they will be useful to you in your communication at work—with each other and with other coworkers and teammates.

    ℥   Centered presence

    ℥   Personal power

    ℥   Clarity of purpose

    ℥   Your behavior style (stabilizer, persuader, etc.)

    ℥   Intent versus impact

    ℥   Contribution versus blame

    ℥   6-Step Checklist

As always, feel free to communicate with me by email or phone anytime.

Thank you both for your energy!

Homework

- ↩ Continue journaling and meditation.

- ↩ Notice when you become uncentered, how you know you're uncentered, and how you re-center yourself.

- ↩ Review your behavior style and Conflict Dynamics Profile (CDP) assessments, and consider how your styles have been at play in your work relationships.

- ↩ Begin reading *The Elephant in the Room,* by Diana McLain Smith.

- ↩ Bring questions for each other to our next joint session.

- ↩ Think through one past difficulty and how you imagine you will handle it differently in the future.

Notes

- ↩ The first part of the session we talked about your reactions to the CDP.

  - Some surprises.
  - Some "of course."
  - Nice if everyone could take the CDP.
  - Some feedback was useful, some not so much.

- ↩ We went over your behavior styles, including what seemed true for each of you, and what you thought the other person needed to know about your preferences. There were some similarities:

  - Your mutual tendency to withdraw/disengage in conflict.
  - Your desire to "get it right."
  - (Name) can be defensive when criticized.
  - (Name) needs to know all the data before making a decision.
  - We did some role-play around offering feedback that might be seen as critical.

ↂ We revisited The Ladder of Inference and the fact that people move up the ladder very quickly in conflict. It's easy to draw conclusions based on our view of the world and then look for more data to confirm those conclusions.

ↂ Both of you reflected that your interactions at work have been going well:

- Easy work and non-work conversations.
- Working more like a team.
  - (Name) is able to be more patient when asked for help.
  - (Name) is pitching in with heavy work load.

ↂ A coworker noticed that things have been lighter and "not so frigid."

ↂ We took a look at some questions about future interactions:

- What is needed to resolve this process so that the solution is sustainable?
- What are problem areas that could get in the way down the line?
- How will you know if there's a problem?
- How would you like to handle minor conflicts so that they don't escalate?

APPENDIX E
6-STEP CHECKLIST WORKSHEET

The following checklist will help guide the parties in holding powerful learning conversations. It can be used before and during the conversation to help keep the purpose clear, the conversation safe, and the preferred outcome in sight.

For help with beginning the conversation, see "Possible Openings" on page 186.

1.   **Center:** How will I remind myself to center before the conversation, and to re-center periodically during the conversation?

2.   **Purpose:** What is my purpose? Is it a useful purpose?

3.   **Inquiry:** What are some honest, open-ended questions I might ask my partner? What do I need to learn about how he or she sees this situation?

4. **Acknowledgment:** What feelings might surface that I can acknowledge? How will I remember to summarize?

5. **Advocacy:** What is my primary message? How will I tell my story while maintaining a respectful and non-judgmental stance?

6. **Move to Action/Build Agreement:** What are possible scenarios my partner might offer? What will I suggest? What is my preferred outcome?

Possible Openings

- I have something I'd like to discuss with you that I think will help us work together better.

- I'd like to talk about _____ with you, but first I'd like to get your point of view.

- I need your help with what just happened. Do you have a few minutes to talk?

- I need your help with _____. Can we talk about it (soon)? If they say, "Sure, let me get back to you," follow up with them.

- I think we have different perceptions about _____. I'd like to hear your thinking on this.

- I've noticed a recurring argument (conflict, disagreement, problem) we seem to have. I'd like to talk about why that happens.

※ I'd like to see if we can reach a better understanding about
_____. I really want to hear your feelings about this
and share my perspective as well.

※ Write your opening in the blank space below:

SAMPLE AGREEMENT

The following agreement is an example of one created by two parties engaged in a process like the one described in this book. I asked questions and facilitated the writing, but they developed the parameters and the language themselves; I merely wrote down their thoughts.

This agreement is specific to these parties, and addresses basic commitments and requests. Your parties will have their own considerations, and your HR department may have a document you can use as well.

Agreement between:

Date:

We, _____ and _____, as employees of _____, are grateful to have engaged with each other in a professional development opportunity offered through our organization, and with the coaching assistance of _____. We have made certain agreements with each other that we would like to express in this document. In addition, we respectfully make requests for support to reinforce the process in future interactions.

We agree to:

ↀ Put forth the effort, energy, and patience toward continuing a healthy work relationship by fully listening and communicating openly about any issue or conflict that arises.

ↀ Express anger—and emotions in general—in a constructive and purposeful way.

ↀ Be open to hearing each other's perspective when we disagree.

ↀ Be respectful and keep an open mind about our own and other coworkers' perspectives.

ↀ Meet monthly, off campus, for one year, for a relationship check-in.

ↀ Meet conflict head-on by holding conversations privately, first putting forth our positive intention, forgiving easily, and assuming positive intent on the part of the other.

ↀ Remember that there are often external factors at play.

ↀ Be grateful for the opportunity any conflict presents to problem solve and strengthen the relationship.

We request of each other:

ↀ Patience, openness, and commitment.

ↀ Specifically:

· _____ requests that _____ be patient and open to hearing a different perspective.

· _____ asks that _____ communicate about conflicts or issues as they arise.

In order to move forward, we respectfully request of our organization that:

ↀ We have a team get-together once a month, contingent upon interest and willingness from coworkers.

❧ We have a ninety-day follow-up session with
_____.

❧ We receive immediate and specific feedback from senior management as appropriate regarding behavior
and work style.

❧ This agreement remains confidential to the parties involved.

Addressing Setbacks

In the course of our work, if the relationship should once
again become adversarial or in danger of reverting to old
behaviors, we will:

❧ Stop immediately and set a time to talk privately.

❧ Acknowledge our individual contributions to the situation and apologize where appropriate.

❧ Revisit this agreement, find the areas we've neglected,
and apply the conflict skills we've acquired through this
program.

❧ Ask senior management for feedback and support.

❧ We understand that frustrations and conflict may and
probably will happen in the natural course of working
together. We promise each other to do our best not to
let those frustrations undermine our positive intentions
as enumerated in this agreement.

Signature   Date

Signature   Date

Further Resources

The following are some of my favorite books, authors, and websites on the topics of conflict, communication, aikido, and personal and organizational effectiveness. I wish you well in your exploration and practice.

Books

Crum, Thomas. *The Magic of Conflict.* New York: Simon & Schuster, 1987.

Crum, Thomas. *Journey to Center.* New York: Simon & Schuster, 1997.

Crum, Thomas. *Three Deep Breaths.* San Francisco: Berrett-Koehler, 2006.

Edmondson Amy C. *Teaming.* San Francisco: John Wiley & Sons, 2012.

Fisher, Roger, and William Ury. *Getting to Yes.* New York: Penguin Books, 1991.

Goldsmith, Marshall. *Triggers.* New York: Penguin Books, 2015.

Goleman, Daniel. *Emotional Intelligence*. New York: Bantam Books, 1997.

Kahane, Adam. *Power and Love: A Theory and Practice of Social Change*. San Francisco: Berrett-Koehler, 2010.

Mindell, Adam. *Metaskills*. Tempe, AZ.: New Falcon Publications, 1995.

Mindell, Arnold. *The Leader as Martial Artist: An Introduction to Deep Democracy*. San Francisco: HarperCollins, 1992.

Mitchell, Barbara, and Cornelia Gamlem. *The Essential Workplace Conflict Handbook*. Wayne, NJ: Career Press, 2015.

Patterson, Kerry, Joseph Grenny, Ron McMillan, and Al Switzler. *Crucial Conversations: Tools for Talking When the Stakes Are High*. New York: McGraw-Hill, 2002.

Pink, Daniel H. *To Sell Is Human*. New York: Penguin Books, 2012.

Ringer, Judy. *Unlikely Teachers: Finding the Hidden Gifts in Daily Conflict*. Portsmouth, NH: OnePoint Press, 2006.

Runde, Craig E., and Tim A. Flanagan. *Developing Your Conflict Competency*. San Francisco: John Wiley & Sons, 2010.

Scott, Kim. *Radical Candor: Be a Kick-Ass Boss Without Losing Your Humanity*. New York: St. Martin's Press, 2017.

Smith, Diana McLain. *The Elephant in the Room: How Relationships Make or Break the Success of Leaders and Organizations*. San Francisco: Wiley/Jossey-Bass, 2011.

Stone, Douglas, Bruce Patton, and Sheila Heen. *Difficult Conversations: How to Discuss What Matters Most*. New York: Viking Penguin, 1999.

Stone, Douglas, and Sheila Heen. *Thanks for the Feedback: The Science and Art of Receiving Feedback Well*. New York: Viking Penguin, 2014.

Ury, William. *The Power of a Positive No*. New York: Bantam Books, 2008.

Warner, Judith S. *From Chaos to Center.* Aspen, CO: Aiki Works, Inc., 1999.

Wise, Will. *Ask Powerful Questions: Create Conversations That Matter.* Highland Park, IL.: Round Table Companies, 2017.

Aikido philosophy, technique, and applications

Bryner, Andy, and Dawna Markova. *An Unused Intelligence.* Berkeley: Conari Press, 1996.

Dobson, Terry. *Aikido in Everyday Life: Giving In to Get Your Way.* Berkeley: North Atlantic Books, 1993.

Leonard, George. *The Way of Aikido, Life Lessons from an American Sensei.* New York: Penguin Books, 2000.

Palmer, Wendy. *The Practice of Freedom: Aikido Principles as a Spiritual Guide.* Berkeley: Rodmell Press, 2002.

Ringer, Judy. *Ki Moments* blog, Portsmouth, NH: OnePoint Press, 2006.

Stevens, John. *The Philosophy of Aikido.* New York: Kodansha International, 2001.

Strozzi-Heckler, John. *Aikido and the New Warrior.* Berkeley: North Atlantic Books, 1985.

Websites, Blogs, and Videos

The following websites and links offer information, books, videos, exercises, newsletters, and excellent articles on aikido, difficult conversations, conflict transformation, and leadership.

Blogs and Videos

Celeste Headlee, "10 Ways to Have a Better Conversation," TED (blog), May 2015, *https://www.ted.com*

Margaret Heffernan, "Dare to Disagree," filmed June 2012 at TED Global, TED video, *https://www.ted.com*

Kathryn Schultz, "On Being Wrong," filmed March 2011, TED video, *https://www.ted.com*

Julian Treasure, "5 Ways to Listen Better," filmed July 2011 at TED Global, TED video, *https://www.ted.com*

Websites

Action Design; The Ladder of Inference:
https://www.actiondesign.com

Aiki Works; Thomas Crum:
http://aikiworks.com

Leadership Embodiment; Wendy Palmer:
http://www.leadershipembodiment.com

Power & Presence; Judy Ringer:
https://www.judyringer.com

Triad Consulting; Difficult Conversations:
http://triadconsultinggroup.com

Vital Smarts; Crucial Conversations:
https://www.vitalsmarts.com

What Is Essential; Public Conversations Project:
https://www.whatisessential.org

Acknowledgments

I begin by acknowledging my first and most significant mentor in the joyful work of bringing aikido to a wide audience—Thomas Crum, and his Aiki Approach. Tom lives his words in all that he does. His pivotal book *The Magic of Conflict* and the many that followed are among the earliest guides for those, like me, who sought to live aikido principles off the mat. He travels a path with heart, giving freely of himself and his work. A deep bow to you, dear friend and sensei. Words can't fully acknowledge the gift of your ki in the world.

Sheila Heen's writing, training, and insight hold a similar place in my heart. Many of the concepts in this book I first encountered reading *Difficult Conversations: How To Discuss What Matters Most*, written by Sheila and her partners, Douglas Stone and Bruce Patton. Since it was first published in 1999, *Difficult Conversations* has inspired a host of similar texts on much-needed practices for communicating consciously and intentionally. She has led the way for many like me, and generously shares her wisdom.

For introducing me to the world of Process Work, thank you Joy Jacobs—teacher and partner in processing the hidden gifts in daily conflict and discovering the "god in the garbage."

For your willingness to share your own best practices when conflict arises in organizations, thank you Connie Roy-Czyzowski, Mea

Allen, Fran Liautaud, Mike Bell, James Warda, and Maureen Connolly. You do this every day.

Countless friends and family members contributed to the publication of this book in ways that range from brainstorming and proofreading to listening, wondering, questioning, and answering calls for support. For all the breakfasts, cups of tea, phone calls, and long walks of encouragement and feedback, I thank Ellen Fineberg, Susan Losapio, Nina Ringer, Debbie Rodin, Cynthia Harriman, Carol Dudley, Janice George, Donna Melillo, Mark Stailey, Melisa Gillis, Jane Wexler, Beth Boynton, and the many readers and contributors to my blog, *Ki Moments,* who offered their energy in finding just the right title!

Thank you to my students and aikido partners at Portsmouth Aikido, Portland Aikido, Framingham Aikikai, and New England Aikikai, especially David Halprin, Aaron Cass, Albert Delaney, and the late Mitsunari Kanai Sensei. What I know of the physical practice of aikido comes from our long association and your love of the art. And to Wendy Palmer, Richard Strozzi-Heckler, and the late George Leonard, thank you for your writing and wisdom, and for spreading the way of aikido throughout the world.

Thank you Janice Molloy, Kara Steere, Sonja Hakala, Vicky Schubert, and B. Lynn Goodwin, editors and thought partners, for getting me started, giving me guidance, and conveying faith and confidence that this book would get out into the world; Barbara Ringer—amazingly talented sister-in-law, artist, photographer, and mom, for somehow always making me look my best; my right arm and trusted assistant Tracie Shroyer, for being there, and for being me when I can't be there myself; and Adam Richardson for his intuitive renderings of aikido in motion. His illustrations bring this book to life.

I'm equally indebted to Michael Pye, senior acquisitions editor at Red Wheel Weiser/Career Press, for your encouragement, support, patience, and incredible design team. You understood the book from the beginning and helped it become its best self. And many thanks to Gina Schenck, for her careful editing and thoughtful book design, and Eryn Carter Eaton and the Career Press publicity team for their constant support.

To coaching and workshop participants, thank you for teaching me day in and day out about the beauty of centered presence and for being allies in the magical transformation that happens when conflict is reframed as opportunity.

Lastly, and most importantly, thank you to my mother, Lorna, for her beautiful heart and unconditional love; to Mike, Debbie, Susan, and Paula for teaching me how to listen; and especially to my husband, Jim, whose continued love and support is key to my success in work and life. Thank you for your willingness to be honest even when it's not easy, for your intelligent editing, and your presence with every doubt, question, and needy request. For showing me how to let go, lower my guard, and learn to be free. And for helping me find my center when I most need it.

INDEX

About the Author

Judy Ringer is the author of *Unlikely Teachers: Finding the Hidden Gifts in Daily Conflict*—a book of stories, practices, and inspiration on turning life's challenges into life teachers—and author and narrator of "Managing Conflict in the Workplace: An Aiki Approach" CD, in which she answers frequently asked questions and offers practical advice about transforming conflict in the workplace.

A skilled vocalist and National Anthem singer, Judy has performed in many venues, including singing The Star Spangled Banner for the Boston Red Sox at Fenway Park. She is the producer of the CDs "Simple Gifts: Making the Most of Life's Ki Moments" and "This Little Light: The Gift of Christmas," in which she narrates stories from her blog and sings familiar standards from the Great American Songbook.

The owner of Power & Presence Training and founder of Portsmouth Aikido, Judy provides conflict, communication, and presentation skills training internationally using principles from the martial art aikido, in which she holds a third-degree black belt.

She's written numerous articles on the relevance and application of the aikido metaphor, including pieces in *The Systems Thinker, SoL North America Journal-Reflections,* and *Aikido Today Magazine.* She publishes widely on the Internet and twice a month through her award-winning newsletter, *Ki Moments.*

Born and raised in the Chicago area, Judy's adopted home is Portsmouth, New Hampshire, where she lives with her husband Jim.